EYEWITNESS
REPTILE

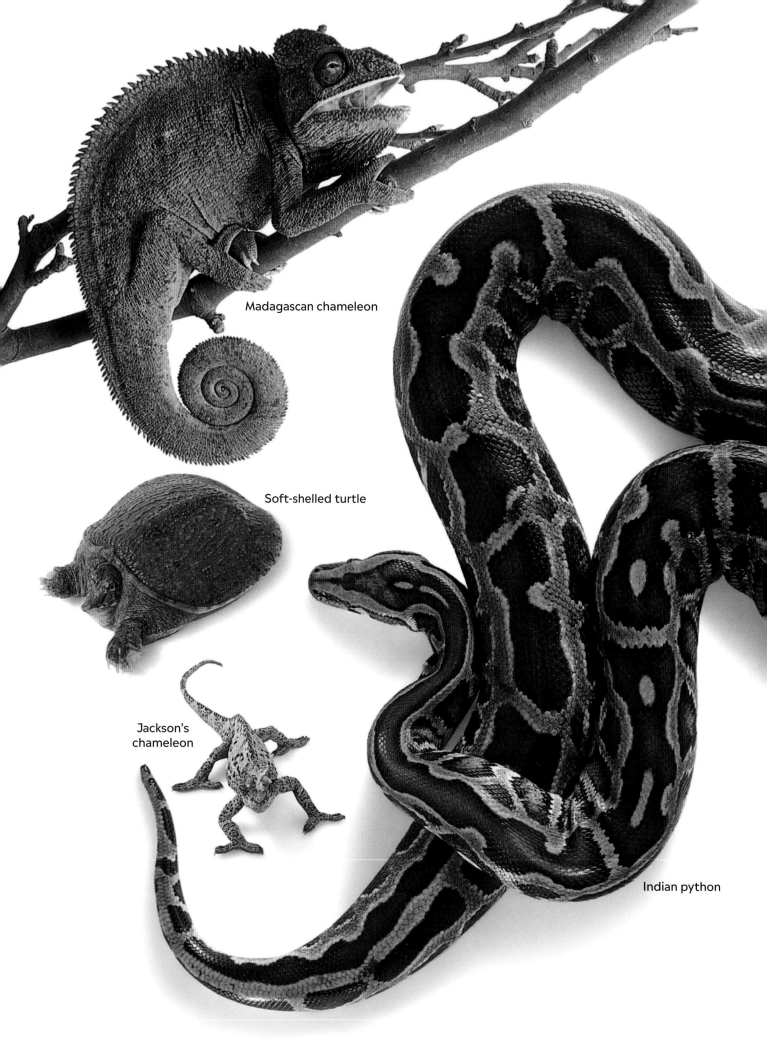

Madagascan chameleon

Soft-shelled turtle

Jackson's chameleon

Indian python

Starred tortoise

Radiated tortoise

EYEWITNESS
REPTILE

Written by
COLIN McCARTHY

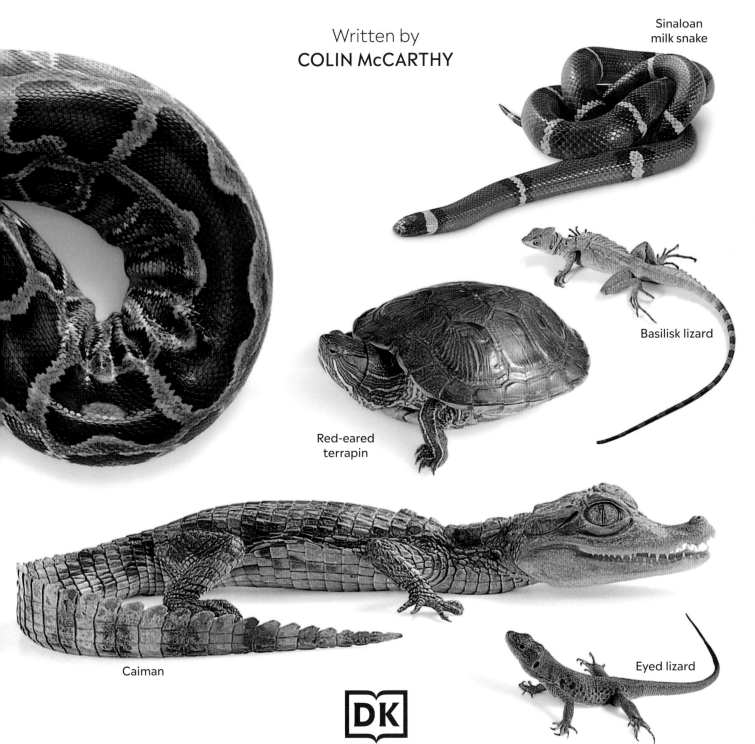

Sinaloan
milk snake

Basilisk lizard

Red-eared
terrapin

Caiman

Eyed lizard

DK

Tree skink

Tegu lizard

Caiman

Grass snake

REVISED EDITION

DK DELHI
Senior Art Editor Vikas Chauhan
Project Editor Upamanyu Das
Editorial team Arpit Aggarwal, Chhavi Nagpal
Art Editor Tanvi Sahu
Assistant Art Editor Prateek Maurya
Assistant Picture Researcher Nunhoih Guite
Managing Editor Kingshuk Ghoshal
Managing Art Editor Govind Mittal
DTP Designers Nand Kishor Acharya, Pawan Kumar, Deepak Mittal
DTP Coordinator Jagtar Singh
Jackets Designer Vidushi Chaudhry
Senior Jackets Coordinator Priyanka Sharma Saddi

DK LONDON
Senior Editor Georgina Palffy
Senior Art Editor Sheila Collins
Project Editor Hélène Hilton
US Senior Editor Kayla Dugger
US Executive Editor Lori Cates Hand
Managing Editor Francesca Baines
Managing Art Editor Philip Letsu
Production Editor Gillian Reid
Production Controller Jack Matts
Senior Jackets Designer Surabhi Wadhwa-Gandhi
Jacket Design Development Manager Sophia MTT
Publisher Andrew Macintyre **Associate Publishing Director** Liz Wheeler
Art Director Karen Self
Publishing Director Jonathan Metcalf

Consultant Colin McCarthy

FIRST EDITION
Project Editors Gillian Denton, Lynne Williams
Art Editor Neville Graham **Senior Editor** Helen Parker
Senior Art Editors Jacquie Gulliver, Julia Harris
Production Louise Barratt **Picture Research** Kathy Lockley
Special Photography Karl Shone, Jane Burton, Kim Taylor, Colin Keates

SECOND EDITION
Revised by David Burnie

This Eyewitness ® Guide has been conceived by Dorling Kindersley Limited and Editions Gallimard

This American Edition, 2023
First American Edition, 1991
Published in the United States by DK Publishing
1745 Broadway, 20th Floor, New York, NY 10019

A catalog record for this book is available from the Library of Congress.
ISBN 978-0-7440-8477-1 (Paperback)
ISBN 978-0-7440-8478-8 (ALB)

DK books are available at special discounts when purchased in bulk for sales promotions, premiums, fund-raising, or educational use. For details, contact: DK Publishing Special Markets, 1745 Broadway, 20th Floor, New York, NY 10019
SpecialSales@dk.com

Printed and bound in China

www.dk.com

Flying snake

Alligator snapping turtle

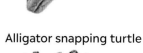

Corn snake

Contents

Rat snake

6
What is a reptile?

8
When reptiles ruled

10
Happy families

12
Inside out

14
Cool customers

16
Uncommon senses

18
Mating displays

20
Examining eggs

22
Spitting images

24
Scale tale

26
Snake selection

28
Lots of lizards

30
Turtles and tortoises

32
Turtle tank

34
Crocodile clan

36
Tuatara

38
A bite to eat

40
A tight squeeze

42
Venomous bite

44
Egg eaters

46
Survival

48
Blending in

50
Lots of legs

52
Ground control

54
Life in trees

56
Waterproofed

58
Natural enemies

60
Just good friends

62
An eye to the future

64
Reptile classification

66
Reptile evolution

68
Threats

70
Glossary

72
Index

What is a **reptile?**

Four groups of reptiles exist today: snakes and lizards, crocodiles and their relatives, turtles and tortoises, and the tuatara. Like fish, birds, mammals, and amphibians, reptiles are vertebrates (have backbones). Reptile young are usually born on land, looking like mini-adults. Scaly skin keeps in moisture, helping them live in dry places, but allows body heat to escape. Therefore, they are known as "cold-blooded" animals, relying on heat from the outside environment to stay warm.

The tegu lizard's tail is made up of bony vertebrae.

Scaly skin

Tegu lizard

Lizards are one of the largest and most varied reptile groups. The tegu lizard (right), mostly found in South America, has skin that is covered with scales that keep in body fluids. Its eyelids are movable, like most other lizards—although some geckos and all snake species cannot blink due to a protective, transparent covering over their eyes. The feet of a reptile give a clue to its lifestyle—the tegu's powerful legs and strong claws propel it through thick rainforest when hunting.

European grass snake with eggs

Laying on land

Most reptiles lay eggs (see pp.20–21), but some give birth to live young. All reptiles that lay eggs do so on land— even turtles that mostly live in water— and in a variety of places, such as sand, grasses, and termite mounds. How long eggs take to hatch depends on the reptile and the climate it lives in.

Extra-long toe for added support

What is not a reptile?

Salamanders look like lizards, but they are amphibians, not reptiles. Amphibians are often mistaken for reptiles, even though they are very different. Amphibians have no scales because they breathe through their skin, and they mostly breed near water before laying eggs in the water. The fire salamander (above) usually found in Europe, keeps her eggs in her body until they hatch, however, and gives birth to tadpoles in shallow water.

Fire salamander

Frogs have glands that produce mucus to stop their skin from drying.

All frogs, such as this tiger-legged monkey frog, are amphibians.

The tail helps with balance.

External ear

Eye with movable eyelid

Reptiles are found on **every continent** except **Antarctica**.

A forked tongue is one of the many special tongue types in reptiles.

15th-century illustration of dragons

Mythical beasts

Reptilelike creatures such as dragons have featured in the mythology of different cultures since the 14th century BCE. Italian explorer Marco Polo recounted seeing dragons (left) on his travels, which were most likely species of flying lizards. In ancient Greek mythology, the multiheaded hydra (right) was a reptilian beast that was hard to kill because it grew two heads when one was cut off.

Hydra

When reptiles **ruled**

Pterosaurs

These flying reptiles ruled the skies for more than 100 million years until they became extinct. Their wings were made of a membrane stretched between a long finger and leg.

Pteranodon, a type of pterosaur, had a wingspan of 23 ft (7 m).

The first reptiles evolved from amphibians more than 300 million years ago (mya) in the Carboniferous Period. But it was not until the Mesozoic Era (252–66 mya) that reptiles ruled life on Earth. While dinosaurs dominated the land, other reptiles reigned over the skies and seas. Their eggs, which had shells and could be laid on dry land, helped reptiles spread across the world.

TIME CHART OF THE EARTH

Paleozoic Era		Mesozoic Era			Cenozoic Era
Carboni-ferous Period	Permian Period	Triassic Period	Jurassic Period	Cretaceous Period	Paleogene, Neogene, and Quaternary periods
359 MYA	299 MYA	252 MYA	201 MYA	145 MYA	66 MYA–PRESENT DAY
Turtles, tortoises, and terrapins					
		Crocodilians			
		Lizards			
		Tuatara			
				Snakes	

Duration of each period not to scale

Ancient giants

The enormous vertebrae or spinal bones (left) of the extinct sea snake *Palaeophis*, found in West Africa, proved that a snake four times larger than a modern python lived in the Cenozoic Era. The vertebrae below are from a present-day 20-ft- (6-m-) long python.

Vertebrae of *Palaeophis*, an ancient sea snake

Vertebrae of a modern python

Skull of crocodilelike reptile *Pelagosaurus*

Slow to change

Lizards first appeared more than 200 mya, evolving alongside dinosaurs. Lizard fossils are rare, but there is evidence (such as below) that different types of lizards, with a body that is typical of lizards today, existed at the end of the Mesozoic Era.

Old crocodiles

Crocodilians (or crocodylomorphs) are as old as dinosaurs, first evolving in the Triassic Period. Their skull (right) has hardly changed over time, but the long, sharp, pointed teeth (below) of early crocodilelike reptiles are more like those of pure fish-eaters—different from the spikelike teeth of modern crocodiles, which eat fish, land animals, and the occasional plant.

Pointed teeth for piercing and eating fish

Doglike jaw

This skull (below), with its doglike jaws, is from the meat-eating reptile *Cynognathus*—an advanced form of the mammal-like reptiles that dominated the land during the Permian and Triassic periods (299–201 mya). Mammals evolved from this group of reptiles about 195 mya.

Large teeth and strong jaw for eating meat

Skull of *Cynognathus*

Turtles first

Turtles are the oldest living reptile group, with fossils dating back around 230 million years. Turtles survived many environmental changes and produced many land and marine forms. Some living species are as small as a tennis ball, but prehistoric turtles could be as big as a car.

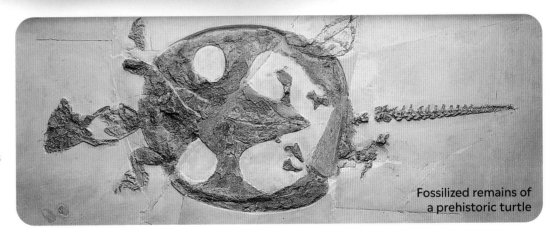

Fossilized remains of a prehistoric turtle

Toothless

A modern turtle skull is unique compared to other vertebrate skulls because it has no openings in the bone for jaw muscles to attach and no teeth. The skull of the Late Triassic turtle *Proganochelys* (left) shows that modern and prehistoric turtle skulls are similar except for evidence of teeth in the old turtle's jaw.

Fossilized *Proganochelys* skull

👁 EYEWITNESS

Mary Anning
British paleontologist Mary Anning (1799–1847) was one of the most famous fossil collectors in history. As a child, she would collect fossils on beaches in Dorset, England. She became an expert at studying fossils at a time when most paleontologists were men. Anning discovered some of the earliest fossils of several prehistoric marine reptiles (such as plesiosaurs and ichthyosaurs).

Snakes

Legless reptiles with long, slender bodies, snakes are split into three groups: primitive snakes (such as pythons and boas), blind snakes (such as thread snakes), and advanced snakes (such as cobras, sea snakes, and vipers). Snakes are found all over the world except in very cold areas and on many islands.

Happy families

Animals are classified according to how they evolved. In the same way that cousins are related because they share the same grandparents, animals with shared ancestors are grouped together. Lizards and snakes are closely related, but crocodiles actually share more ancestry with birds than they do with other reptiles. However, a lack of evidence about ancestors means that groupings are also based on shared features.

Royal python

Patterned scales provide camouflage in the python's grassland and forest habitats.

REPTILES TODAY

Four main groups of reptiles are still alive today. The largest group, lizards and snakes, is sometimes shown as two separate groups.

	Lizards 7,511 species
	Snakes 4,038 species
	Turtles 363 species
	Crocodilians 27 species
	Tuatara 1 species

Number of reptile species alive today

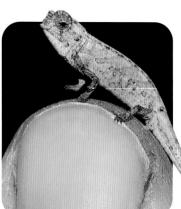

Largest and smallest

The world's smallest known reptile is the nano-chameleon from Madagascar. Male nano-chameleons are around 0.87 in (22 mm) long, including the tail. The world's largest reptile is the estuarine, or saltwater, crocodile, found from southern India to northern Australia. It usually grows to a length of 16 ft (5 m), but there are records of some crocodiles growing longer than 20 ft (6 m).

Nano-chameleon

Estuarine crocodile

The tail is used to propel the caiman through water.

Lizards

Within each reptile group, some species are more closely related than others. Iguanas, agamas, and chameleons are closely related, while geckos form the most primitive (least evolved) lizard group. Monitor lizards, beaded lizards, and glass lizards are also grouped together.

Monitor lizard

Caiman

Crocodilians

This very old group of reptiles is divided into three families: crocodiles, gharials, and alligators (which includes caimans). Crocodilians are, in many ways, a more advanced group than other reptiles— their blood circulation system is more efficient, they are thought to have a more intelligent brain, and they show greater care for their young.

U-shaped upper jaw

Turtles and tortoises

Turtles have short, broad bodies that are enclosed in a bony shell, usually covered by horny plates and sometimes leathery skin. They are divided into two groups based on how the neck bends as it retreats into the shell: hidden-neck turtles (such as tortoises) and side-necked turtles (such as African mud turtles).

Hermann's tortoise

👁 EYEWITNESS

Varad Giri
Indian herpetologist (reptile and amphibian expert) Varad Giri worked as a researcher at the Bombay Natural History Society for more than 10 years. He has discovered 56 new species of reptiles and amphibians in India's Western Ghats. Giri has also helped conserve lizards in the region.

Inside **out**

The bones of many reptiles keep growing throughout their lives, causing some—such as pythons, crocodiles, and giant tortoises—to become giant-sized. While mammals lose their teeth when they are old, most reptiles shed and grow new ones throughout their life.

Tail vertebra

Snakes

The snake's flexible backbone and powerful trunk muscles enable the well-known "serpentine movement." Its vertebrae are strengthened to take the strain from the hard-working muscles. Some smaller snakes have 180 vertebrae along their backbones and longer species can have up to 400. A snake's upper and lower jaws are only loosely connected, making the mouth stretchy.

Trunk vertebra

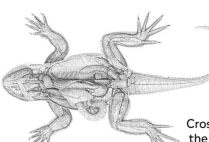

Cross-section of the insides of a lizard

Chameleons

Like many lizards, the chameleon has a highly specialized skeleton. It is adapted for life in trees and bushes. It has a narrow body, which provides stability when its weight is centered on narrow twigs. A chameleon's fingers and toes are good at grasping and its tail can wrap around twigs with a tight grip.

Skull

Ribs

Chameleon skeleton

Three outside toes and two inside toes on each foot help grip branches.

Tail vertebra

Caimans

A long skull with high-set eyes and nostrils allows a caiman to float with just its nose and eyes above the water. It has two pairs of short legs on its long body, with partly webbed toes—five on the front feet, four on the back. Like all crocodilians, its upper jaw is almost solid bone.

Skull

Caiman skeleton

Neck vertebra

Ribs

Python skeleton

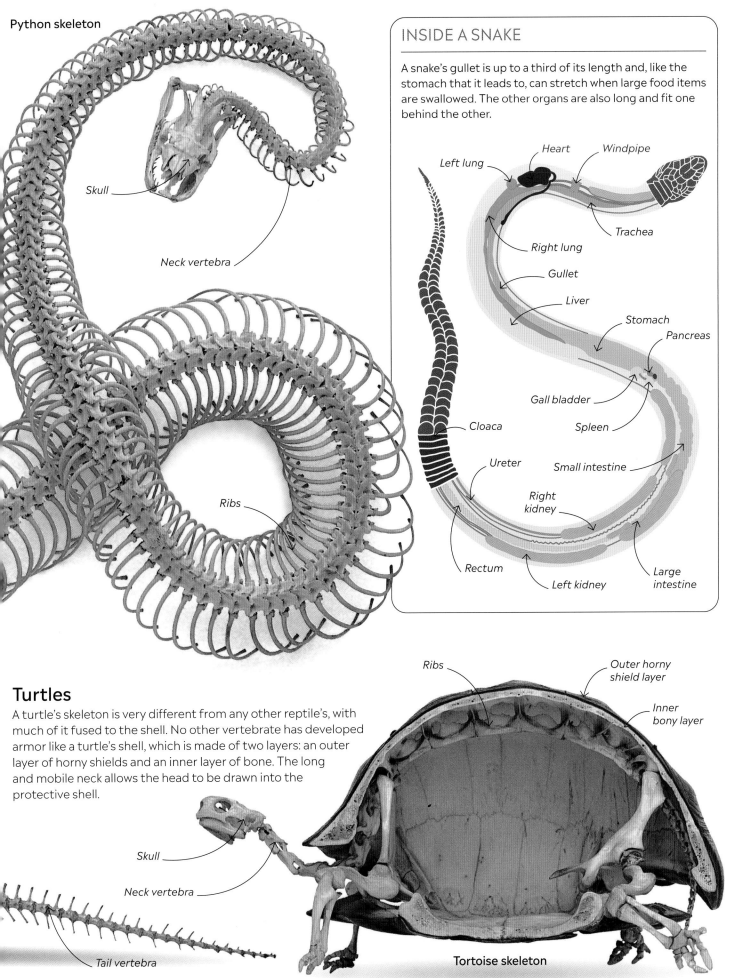

Skull

Neck vertebra

Ribs

INSIDE A SNAKE

A snake's gullet is up to a third of its length and, like the stomach that it leads to, can stretch when large food items are swallowed. The other organs are also long and fit one behind the other.

Left lung

Heart

Windpipe

Right lung

Trachea

Gullet

Liver

Stomach

Pancreas

Gall bladder

Spleen

Cloaca

Ureter

Small intestine

Right kidney

Rectum

Left kidney

Large intestine

Turtles

A turtle's skeleton is very different from any other reptile's, with much of it fused to the shell. No other vertebrate has developed armor like a turtle's shell, which is made of two layers: an outer layer of horny shields and an inner layer of bone. The long and mobile neck allows the head to be drawn into the protective shell.

Ribs

Outer horny shield layer

Inner bony layer

Skull

Neck vertebra

Tail vertebra

Tortoise skeleton

13

Cool customers

Reptiles are cold-blooded (see pp.6–7)—their body temperature changes with that of their surroundings. To be active and able to function, they must be warm—in fact, high temperatures are needed for them to digest food—so they thrive in hot climates. On chilly mornings, reptiles bask in sunshine to warm up. When the day gets hot, they move into the shade to cool down. By moving in and out of the sunshine, their internal temperature stays constant. Low temperatures make reptiles slow and come under threat from predators.

Taking it easy
Crocodiles cool down by opening their mouths to let moisture evaporate or by lying in cool water. American crocodiles lie in burrows when the heat is too much.

Agama lizard seeking shade under a rock

Seeking warmth and shade
In the early morning, the agama lizard sits in the sunshine (above). When the day gets hot, it cools down in the shade (left). This pattern of warming and cooling varies with the seasons. During the cooler months, reptiles are only active at midday, when it is warm. In the summer, they may go underground at midday to avoid overheating.

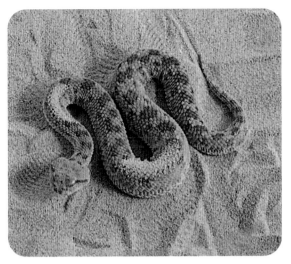

Taking cover

Like many other desert snakes, the sand viper (left and below) avoids the heat of the day. It is mainly nocturnal and sinks itself in the sand if caught in hot sunshine. It moves in a "sidewinding" fashion (see p.53), and may travel up to 0.6 miles (1 km) while hunting for small mammals and lizards.

The snake leaves visible marks as it moves in the sand.

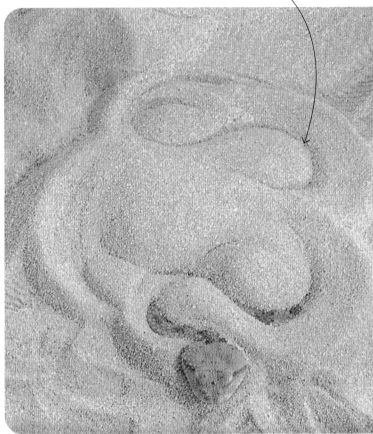

1 Going ...

A sand viper retreats into the sand tail first, wriggling as it goes. Its eyes are well protected from irritating grains of sand by the transparent covering that shields them.

2 Going ...

Shuffling and rocking, the snake descends vertically, shoveling sand up and over its back. Its scales help work the grains of sand along its body to cover it.

3 Gone!

The sand viper is almost completely buried. Soon, only the top of its head will be visible. Bedding down in the hot desert sand protects it from the scorching sunshine and also makes a perfect hiding place when either enemies or prey are nearby.

Thermal dance

To avoid overheating, the shovel-snouted lizard (right) exhibits unusual behavior in temperatures higher than 104°F (40°C). The lizard performs a "dance," balancing on its tail and lifting alternate legs to cool them. It also dives into the sand to cool down.

The lizard lifts a front leg and the opposite hind leg alternately to cool down.

Uncommon senses

Reptiles use smell, sight, and hearing to find out about their surroundings. Some reptiles have additional "senses." Snakes and some lizards "smell" using their tongue and special sensory cells called the Jacobson's organ. Certain snakes are sensitive to infrared heat, which means they can detect warm-blooded prey in the dark. A few reptiles, however, have underdeveloped senses—burrowing reptiles have poor eyesight, and snakes cannot hear very well.

Alligator roar

Alligators communicate over vast distances by bellowing. The sound can be very loud—up to 92 decibels at 16 ft (5 m), which is roughly as loud as the propeller engine of a small airplane.

Swiveling eye is set on a turret.

Eyelids can close to tiny peepholes.

Special toes grasp branches like pincers.

Small but noisy

Most geckos have a voice. Some chirp and click, usually when mating or defending territory. When distressed, some geckos produce high-frequency sounds to ward off predators.

Broad horizons

The chameleon (above) has a wide field of vision and can move each eye independently. If it sees a fly, it can keep one eye pointed at it while the other eye scans the area for enemies as the chameleon moves toward the fly to capture it. Once close, the chameleon swivels both eyes toward the fly to see it with a binocular vision similar to humans'. With both eyes fixed on the fly, the chameleon can pinpoint its position and aim its tongue to catch it.

A story of senses

Like all animals, snakes have evolved over millions of years. At some point, they went through a burrowing stage, which affected their senses—their sight and hearing became weak. Snakes today have no external ears, and vibrations have to move through the skull bone to get to the inner ear. Some snakes, like this Indian python (right), have special heat sensors for detecting warm-blooded prey.

Music to its ears

For thousands of years, snakes have been shown dancing to the music of a charmer's pipe. This led to the belief that snakes are hypnotized by music, while in fact, the snake rises in defense and follows the pipe's movement to attack it.

Deeply forked tongue

Small holes called pit organs help the python sense the heat given off by prey, which is especially helpful in low-light conditions.

TESTING THE AIR

All lizards have a well-developed, extendable tongue, and snakes (right) and monitor lizards have forked tongues. The forked tongue flicks in and out, "tasting" chemical particles that it transfers to the Jacobson's organ in the roof of the mouth. The organ partly "smells" and partly "tastes" the particles to help the reptile follow prey, find a mate, and detect enemies.

Nostril

Tongue

Jacobson's organ

Tear duct

Green snake

A transparent eyelid wipes the eye clean.

An iguana's ear can pick up low frequencies not audible to humans.

Sight and sound

Iguanas have very good eyesight. They can see in color, which explains why many communicate with their colorful head ornaments, crests, and throat fans. Color is important in many lizards, as it is a way of distinguishing males from females. Iguanas also have good hearing. While snakes mainly hear vibrations from the ground through their skull bones, most lizards can hear airborne sounds through visible ear openings, in which the eardrum sits close to the surface.

Mating season

Giant tortoises (above) are capable of mating throughout the year but mostly do so from January to May. The male will often show interest by ramming the female in the side with his shell. The act of mating can take several hours.

Mating displays

Reptiles spend most of their days adjusting their body temperature, searching for food, and escaping from predators. But in the mating season, they also need to attract a mate in order to reproduce. Male lizards often display bright colors to appeal to females, and some also show off elaborate frills and crests. These same displays are also used to warn off male rivals.

Flashy animals

The male frigate bird (above) and the anole lizard (right) both attract mates by inflating their pouch.

A couple of swells

Male anole lizards (below and right) inflate their reddish throat sacs as a sign of aggression toward other males. Two same-sized lizards may flaunt their throat sacs at one another for hours, while a smaller lizard would instantly retreat. There are many different species of anole lizard, which live in the tropical areas of South and Central America. They have the ability to change from green to different shades of brown.

The flap of skin under the throat is called a dewlap.

Special storage

Many female snakes can store sperm in some cases for months or even years after they have mated. This means that, when there is lots of food to feed the young and conditions are favorable, the snakes can use the stored sperm to fertilize more eggs to produce more young.

👁 EYEWITNESS

Charles Carpenter
US zoologist Charles Carpenter (1921–2016) studied how some reptiles behave during mating—from combat rituals among male speckled kingsnakes to breeding habits in fox snakes. Carpenter's anole lizard is named after him.

Mating dance

Once a male snake has found a female, he stimulates her into mating by rubbing his chin along her back while their bodies and tails intertwine. During the mating season, two male snakes will sometimes perform a kind of combat dance as they vie for a favored female. Snakes may often avoid fighting by signaling their intentions from a distance, proving which creature is superior without having to fight.

Test of strength

Male monitor lizards (above) rear up and wrestle at the start of the mating season. The weaker animal usually gives up before it is injured.

Snakes can stay entwined for hours while mating.

Examining eggs

Most young reptiles develop inside an egg, cushioned in a bag of fluid called the amnion. Many reptile eggs have a soft, flexible shell, although some have hard shells. Oxygen and moisture are passed to the young through the shell, and the yolk provides food.

Underground
This strange-looking egg was laid by a ground python, a burrowing snake from West Africa. The egg is large in proportion to the mother—an 33-in- (85-cm-) long female may lay eggs 4 in (12 cm) in length.

Mother love
The female Indian python coils around her 30 or so leathery-shelled eggs and twitches her muscles to warm the eggs.

Snakes
Most snake eggs have parchmentlike shells. The young hatch by using a special, sharp egg tooth to break the shell. Most snakes bury their eggs. However, some are viviparous— they give birth to live young, not eggs.

Common as muck
The common African house snake often lays eight to 10 eggs in manure heaps or termite mounds.

Lizards
Most lizard eggs have leathery shells— except geckos, which lay hard-shelled eggs. Most lizards ignore their eggs once laid, but some skinks return to brood, warming the eggs with their bodies.

Nest intruders
The female Nile monitor lizard prefers to lay her 40–60 eggs in a termite mound. The heat inside the mound incubates the eggs.

Buried alive
While some chameleons give birth to live young, Parson's chameleon lays 30–40 eggs in a hole in the ground. It fills the hole to protect its eggs, which can take up to 20 months to hatch.

Stuck on you
The tokay gecko, like many geckos and skinks, lays eggs two at a time. They are soft and sticky at first, but soon harden and stick to the surface on which they were laid.

Spindle eggs
The eggs of the Javan bloodsucker lizard are a peculiar spindle shape. It is not clear why—species closely related to it have oval eggs.

Turtles and tortoises

Tortoises and some turtles lay hard-shelled eggs, while marine and some river turtles lay soft ones. Most dig a hole for their eggs and may return to the same spot every year. The sex of the baby can be decided by the temperature during incubation.

Matamata
The eggs of this strange South American turtle look like ping-pong balls. Like all aquatic turtles, the female matamata must leave the water to lay her eggs.

Spur-thighed tortoise
The female spur-thighed tortoise lays approximately four to 10 eggs in a nest in soil. She may do this twice in one summer. The small eggs have hard shells.

Gentle giant
The Galápagos giant tortoise is one of the world's biggest. It lays eggs in sun-baked soil, where they incubate for up to 200 days. Many are destroyed by foraging rats and pigs, which were brought to the island by settlers.

Snake-necked turtle
The Australian snake-necked turtle leaves the water at night, after rainfall, to lay eggs in a hole nest on land.

PROTECTIVE EGGS

Reptilian eggs are made up of layers. Under a brittle outer shell is a flexible inner layer, inside which the fluid-filled amnion houses the embryo. The yolk supplies food to the baby.

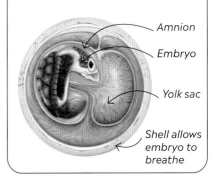

Amnion

Embryo

Yolk sac

Shell allows embryo to breathe

Mass nesting
Every year, Olive Ridley sea turtles arrive on tropical beaches during very high tides. Each female digs a hole, lays 100 eggs, then returns to the sea.

Crocodilians

Caimans and alligators make mounds of fresh vegetation, soil, and leaf litter for their hard-shelled eggs. Crocodiles and gharials make hole nests at beaches and in dry, crumbly soil. The female often stays close by to fend off egg thieves. All crocodilian eggs have to be kept warm; the sex of the hatchling is decided by the temperature of the egg in early incubation.

Alligator egg

Safely nestled
The female African dwarf crocodile lays 20 eggs in a specially made mound nest. The female American alligator, however, lays as many as 35–50 eggs in a nest. When the eggs are ready to hatch, the mother tears open the nest to let the hatchlings out.

Dwarf crocodile egg

Spitting images

Baby reptiles are smaller, similar-looking versions of their adult selves. They have the ability to fend for themselves. This is necessary because most reptile parents leave their eggs once they are laid—although some lizards and snakes do protect them, and some watch over their young. Baby reptiles are able to both feed themselves and survive in the environment that they'll inhabit once they're mature. A young reptile's eating habits are different from an adult's; for example, a young crocodile can survive on insects, but as it grows, it will need larger meals.

Young caiman

Like mother, like daughter

A young caiman (left) is born fully formed and able to fend for itself. Like the young alligator (above), it will stay close to its mother for a few weeks, sometimes using her as a basking platform. But at the first sign of danger, it will dive underwater for cover.

Hatching out

Snake eggs often swell and get heavier as they absorb moisture from their surroundings. The time they take to hatch depends on temperature—the warmer it is, the faster the eggs develop. So the mother will often lay her eggs in a place that is warm and slightly moist, such as compost heaps, where rotting vegetation produces heat. Often, the baby snake is much longer than the egg it hatched from—inside the egg, its whole body was tightly coiled.

1 The egg
This is the egg of a North American rat snake, which mates in spring and fall. A few weeks later the female lays between five and 30 soft-shelled, oval eggs.

4 Making a move
When it decides to leave the egg, the snake does so quickly and slithers along in the normal snakelike way (see p.53). However, if a snake is removed from its egg a little too early, it will writhe around, unable to move along properly. It therefore seems likely that the snake only becomes fully coordinated just before hatching.

Live birth
The adder, Britain's only venomous snake, produces six to 20 live young that are incubated inside the mother and are born in August or September.

Looks can deceive

Most geckos lay their eggs between pieces of bark or stick them to a wall. The female sandstone gecko (right) lays her eggs in rock crevices. Because they are exposed to the elements, the eggs have hard shells (see pp.20–21). Although many geckos lay their eggs in shared sites, they don't take care of their young at all—in fact, it is unusual to see mother and young as close as seen here. The young are independent from birth but are not able to reproduce until the age of 18 months.

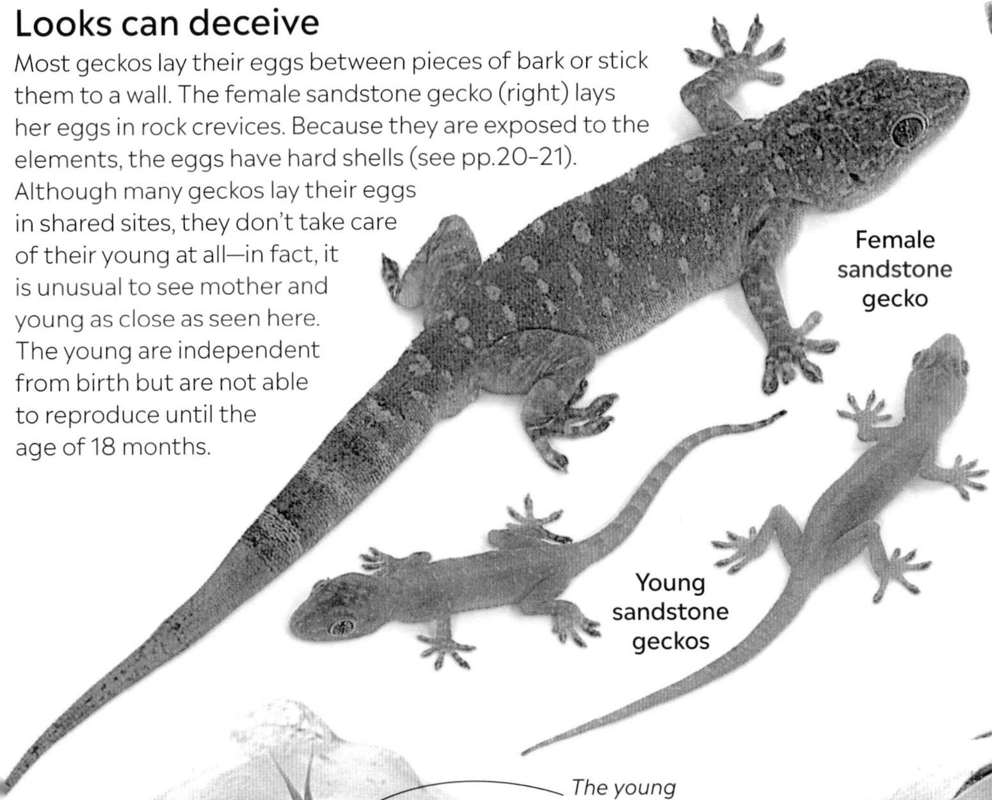

Female sandstone gecko

Young sandstone geckos

Hazards of hatching

Among reptiles, turtles lay the most eggs but care for them the least. Abandoned to the sand in which its egg was buried, this little hatchling (above) will fight alone to survive in the world.

The young snake checks its surroundings with its tongue.

The snake is in no hurry to leave the safety of its shell.

2 Breaking the shell

During the seven to 15 weeks it takes to develop inside the egg, the young rat snake gets nourishment from the yolk. A day or two before hatching, the yolk sac is drawn into the body, and the yolk is absorbed into the snake's intestine. As the young snake develops, a sharp but temporary "egg tooth" grows from the tip of its upper jaw. The baby snake uses this to pierce the egg shell and get its first view of the world.

3 Leaving the egg

Having tested its surroundings by flicking its tongue in and out (see p.17), the young snake cautiously leaves its shell. It will be in no hurry to leave and may stay with only its head poking out for a day or two. That way, if disturbed, it can always go back inside the egg.

5 Minor miracle

Fully out of its shell now, it seems amazing that such a long snake could ever have been packed inside such a small egg. The hatchlings, at 11–16 in (28–40 cm) long, may be up to seven times longer than their egg.

Scale tale

Skin forms a barrier between the outside world and our internal tissues. Reptile skin is dry and scaly—the scales on the outer layer are made of a fibrous protein called keratin. The outer skin is shed and renewed by cells in the inner layer. This allows snakes to grow and replaces worn-out skin. Lizards and snakes have a "sloughing" time when they shed their skin. Most lizards shed skin in large flakes over a few days, while snakes slough the entire skin in one go.

Old skin is fragile and can break easily.

Skin deep

Reptile skin varies from one species to another. In some lizards, it may be bumpy, raised in spines, or form crests. In most snakes, the belly scales form wide, overlapping plates, which help it move (see p.53).

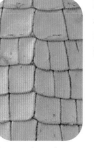

Caiman back

Smooth caiman belly skin

Horny-skinned armor
A caiman's back and tail has rough, bony scales (scutes) strengthened by bony plates.

On the crest
Chameleon scales rise to a crest on its back.

Diggers
This skink has smooth scales that stop mud from clinging.

Plated lizard
This lizard has bony plates under its scales.

COUNTING SNAKE SCALES

Examining the pattern and count of a snake's scales can help identify the species. Scale counts are mostly taken at the middle of the body, where the number of rows is often highest. Cobras, however, may have more scale rows at the neck because the skin there expands when the cobra spreads its hood.

Dorsal (back and side) scales

Ventral (underside) scales on pythons and boas

Ventral scales on colubrid snakes—the largest snake family

New skin is smooth and shiny.

New for old

Like reptiles, insects and other arthropods molt or shed their tough outer skins, or exoskeletons, so they can grow. This cicada (right) has almost finished its final molt, transforming into an adult cicada with working wings. Its new exoskeleton is soft but hardens quickly.

Wings expand as fluid is pumped into them.

Sloughing

The slow worm is a European legless lizard that sheds its skin in large pieces about four times a year. Adult lizards molt once a month when they are most active. Some lizards pull off their old skin with their mouth and swallow the strips, but the slow worm peels it off, like a snake. Most reptiles shed their skin throughout their lives because they never stop growing.

Renewing the rattle

A rattlesnake's tail is made up of hollow segments of keratin. Every time the snake sheds its skin, a new segment is added to the rattle. When the tail shakes, the segments knock together to produce the rattle sound.

The rattle is used to warn off potential aggressors.

All in the eye

Several days before a snake sheds its skin, its eyes look cloudy, its skin is dull, it loses its appetite, and it may turn aggressive. Many snakes look for water to replace the body fluids they lose with their skins.

New skin for old

Snakes have no limbs, so they are able to slither out of their old skin within half an hour and leave it behind in one piece. The sloughing starts along the lips—the snake rubs its head on the ground to turn the skin back, then slithers out, turning the skin inside out as it does so. The snake emerges, glistening in its new colors and scales.

Top

Adult rat snake skin

Underside

Young snakes shed skin soon after they hatch and about seven times in their first year.

Young rat snake skin

Snake selection

Snakes have no legs, eyelids, or eardrums, but can move quickly and sense their surroundings with special sensors. They live both in water and on land on all continents except Antarctica.

Bottoms up

When threatened, this burrowing snake (right) hides its head under its coiled body. It then waves its tail and shoots blood-stained liquid from its anal opening.

A snake's coloration can vary according to its age.

Back biter

This mildly venomous Madagascan hognose snake (right) has fangs at the back of its jaw. It rarely bites people, but if threatened, it flattens its neck (like a cobra) and hisses loudly. It shelters in burrows in grassland areas, eats small mammals and amphibians, and grows up to 5 ft (152 cm) long.

Corny

This nonvenomous American snake (above) is called the corn snake due to checkered markings on its belly that look like grain patterns on some types of corn. The longest corn snake measured was 72 in (183 cm).

Shrinking violet

This shy, gray-banded kingsnake (below) is rarely seen in the wild but is a popular pet. It is 47 in (121 cm) when fully grown and lives on a diet of lizards.

These snakes can grow 40 in (102 cm) long.

Night prowler

The Californian mountain kingsnake (above) is another snake that is harmless to people. In warm weather, it rests during the day and hunts at night for lizards, other snakes, and young birds.

This kind of color patterning in kingsnakes is called "blairi."

Stock still

The vine snake of Southeast Asia (above) spends hours hanging in trees, motionless and camouflaged. Its forward-facing eyes give it binocular vision, which helps it judge distances, especially when lunging at lizards.

Eyes face forward.

The pits

The North American copperhead (above) is a member of the pit viper family. Like its rattlesnake relatives, the copperhead has a nasty bite. Its venom enters its victim's bloodstream, causing internal bleeding. However, people rarely die from the bites.

Begone!

There are no snakes in Ireland. According to one legend, St. Patrick banished them to rid the country of evil.

Double bluff

This harmless Sinaloan milk snake (right) looks a lot like the highly venomous coral snake, deterring predators from eating it. Milk snakes are so called due to a mistaken belief that they steal milk from cows.

High flier

The flying snake (above) is a rapid-moving tree snake from southern Asia. It hangs high up in the trees of thick forests, hunting for lizards and frogs. It jumps between branches and glides through the air. When it reaches the lower branches, it flattens its body to increase air resistance and slow down.

👁 EYEWITNESS

María Elena Barragán-Paladines

Ecuadorian conservationist María Elena Barragán-Paladines (holding the tube, right) heads an organization called the Gustavo Orcés Herpetological Foundation, which works to protect the reptiles and amphibians of Ecuador. She has traveled across her country, training people to recognize venomous snakes in order to reduce deaths and injuries from snakebites, while also protecting snake species.

Crest tale

The common iguana's crest runs like the teeth of a comb down the center of its back. Common iguanas are often seen basking in trees.

Mild moloch

The fierce-looking moloch (above) is a harmless, ant-eating lizard. Its spikes deter predators and collect dew, which condenses and runs into the lizard's mouth. It can then live for weeks without drinking.

Lots of lizards

There are more than 7,500 species of lizard, including geckos, iguanas, chameleons, skinks, and monitors. It is the most successful reptile group, having evolved many lifestyles—with lizards living on the ground, in trees, in water, and as burrowers.

Chameleons feed mostly on insects such as crickets.

Komodo king

The world's largest living lizard, the Komodo dragon, is a species of monitor lizard found only on a few Indonesian islands. Some Komodo dragons may grow to lengths of 10 ft (3 m).

Blue mover

The blue-tongued skink (above) constantly flicks its blue tongue in and out. It gives birth to live young and can move fast when necessary.

Armor-plated

Plated lizards (above) have bony plates under their scales. They normally have long tails, but like most other lizards, can shed them to avoid capture (see p.47). This one's tail is regrowing.

Tongue, toes, and tail

This panther chameleon (below) has a sticky-tipped tongue that it can shoot out farther the length of its body to catch its prey. Chameleons also have remarkable toes, which are arranged in a way that helps them clasp tree branches securely, while their tail twines itself around twigs for extra support.

Tree creeper

The glossy-skinned emerald tree skink (left) lives in trees in Indonesia, rarely venturing to the ground.

Blinking gecko

Unlike most geckos, which have a transparent scale over each eye, the leopard gecko (above) can blink. They are mainly ground dwellers and don't have sticky toe pads for climbing.

Color-conscious

Chameleons' main defense against enemies is the ability to change color. The male Jackson's chameleon (right) also has three-pronged horns to help frighten away some foes.

The tip of a **chameleon's tongue** accelerates up to **five times faster** than a **fighter jet**.

Flat as a pancake

The African lizard (below) has a flat body for slipping into crevices and thick, protective scales. It jams itself into a rock crack and inflates its body so that predators can't pry it out.

Eyed lizard

The eyed, or ocellated, lizard (right) from Europe and North Africa can reach lengths of up to 2.6 ft (80 cm). It is a ground dweller, but it can also climb well.

Turtles and tortoises

Reptiles with shells, known as chelonians, are found in most parts of the world. The shell protects and camouflages them. So far, 363 species have been identified, living in saltwater and freshwater habitats and on land. Water-dwelling chelonians are called turtles (pond and river dwellers are sometimes called terrapins), and the rest are tortoises.

Turtle god
In Hindu mythology, the turtle Kurma, an incarnation of the God Vishnu, helped save all life after a flood.

Galápagos giants
In 1835, Charles Darwin wrote about how giant tortoises had adapted to life on the Galápagos Islands. There are two main groups: saddlebacks, which reach up to eat vegetation, and domeshells, which graze on the ground.

The shell is made of 59 to 61 bones and is in two parts: the plastron and the carapace.

The red stripe may fade with old age.

Red ears
Red-eared terrapins, such as the one above, have a broad red stripe on the side of the head. They are gentle, attractive creatures that live in ponds and rivers in the United States. These terrapins climb onto logs to bask in the sunshine, where they may pile up on top of each other. The males have longer claws on their front feet than the females.

Giant tortoises can live for as long as 250 years.

Dealing with pressure

The European pond terrapin (left) lives in Europe, western Asia, and northwest Africa. Pond terrapins are mainly vegetarian and spend most of their time in water. In some pond terrapins from southern Asia, their lungs are encased in bony boxes on the inside of the shell. This protects the lungs from the increased pressure underwater when the animals dive to great depths.

Soft-shelled hunters

The shell of soft-shelled turtles (right) has no horny plates and feels like leather. In Africa, Asia, and North America, the soft-shelled turtles are usually found buried in mud in rivers and ponds. By stretching their long necks to the water's surface, they can breathe through a snorkel-like nose. They hide from enemies but are fierce hunters capable of striking at lightning speeds.

Lonesome George

A giant Pinta Island tortoise named Lonesome George was relocated to Santa Cruz Island in the Galápagos Islands after it appeared to be the last remaining member of its subspecies. Attempts to find a female failed, and George died alone in 2012, aged around 90 years.

Record reptile

Leatherbacks (right) are the largest living turtles. They breed in the Caribbean Sea, then follow jellyfish, their main food, across the Atlantic Ocean. The largest recorded leatherback turtle, which weighed 2,016 lb (914 kg), was found near Harlech, Wales in 1988.

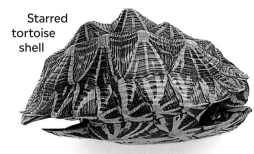

Starred tortoise shell

Hawksbill turtle shell

Radiated tortoise shell

Different shells

Different lifestyles lead to different shells. Land tortoise shells are high-domed (such as the radiated tortoise) or knobby (such as the starred tortoise) to protect from predators' jaws. Turtles (such as the hawksbill turtle) have streamlined shells for moving through water. Soft-shelled turtles have the flattest shells, allowing them to hide in mud.

Turtle tank

In folklore, the alligator snapping turtle was thought to be a cross between a common turtle and an alligator. It is a ferocious turtle with a powerful head and knifelike jaws that spends nearly all its time in water. When fishing for prey, the turtle lies motionless on the river bed with its mouth open. It will eat anything it can catch—snails, clams, and even other turtles. It is one of the world's largest freshwater turtles, growing up to 26 in (66 cm) long and weighing up to 200 lb (91 kg).

The **sharp bite** of an alligator snapping turtle has enough **force** to **snap** human **bones**.

Ridged and roughened shell provides both protection and camouflage.

Wormlike appendage

Sharp jaws used to cut prey

Wiggly worm

One of the most remarkable features of the alligator snapper is the wormlike appendage on the end of its tongue. This fills with blood that colors it red so it looks like an earthworm (right). When hungry, the turtle lies still on the river bed, opens its mouth, and wiggles the "worm." Unwary prey are lured in by this bait, only to find the turtle's powerful jaws snapping shut on them.

The turtle rises on its forelegs when threatened.

32

The matamata's neck is covered in warts and ridges.

Sucked to death

The matamata turtle from South America, like the alligator snapper, lies on river beds waiting for prey. When prey approaches, the matamata expands its throat, creating a current that sucks the prey into its jaws.

Hidden predator

The alligator snapping turtle, found in the southeastern US, looks like a stone, especially when its ridged shell is covered by algae. It relies on this camouflage to stay hidden from any unsuspecting prey before trapping them with its strong forelegs and bladelike jaws. The illegal trafficking of this reptile and the destruction of its habitats have reduced its numbers in the wild, making it an endangered species.

Very powerful forelegs are often used to hold prey.

Crocodile **clan**

Crocodiles, along with their alligator, caiman, and gharial relatives, are descended from the same group as dinosaurs. Crocodilians spend a lot of time basking or lying in water, but can move tremendously fast to attack with power and precision. These ferocious creatures take care of their young more than any other type of reptile.

Gharial skull (top view)

Gharial skull (side view)

Crocodile god

Sobek, the crocodile god of ancient Egypt, was a powerful deity who ruled over rivers and lakes. Shown as a crocodile here, he was sometimes given a human body.

A stitch in time

Mary, Queen of Scots, was held prisoner by English Queen Elizabeth I from 1569 to 1584. Mary and her jailer embroidered a large hanging with panels of animals, including this crocodile (below), presumably to keep her calm as she awaited her execution. The crocodile is just one of the many examples they produced.

Steve Irwin

Steve Irwin (1962–2006) was an Australian wildlife conservationist and educator. He caught his first venomous snake at the age of 6, and by 9 years old, he was catching small crocodiles. Irwin went on to host a wildlife documentary on crocodiles, which later turned into the hit TV series *The Crocodile Hunter*. Wildlife lovers around the world watched him and his wife Terri capture and relocate large crocodiles to Australian national parks.

Egyptian mummies

In ancient Egypt, crocodiles were sacred and were looked after in temples of Sobek, draped with gold. When they died, they were mummified (below).

Gharials

Strangest of all the crocodilians, the gharial has a long, narrow snout with small, piercing teeth. The snout sweeps through the water, and the interlocking, outward-pointing teeth grasp fish. The adult male wards off rivals with a loud buzz, made by breathing out through a bump on his nose.

Caimans

Caimans have short, broad snouts and are part of the alligator family. Young caimans eat insects and switch to eating water snails, fish, mammals, and birds as they grow. One broad-snouted species is particularly adaptable and has been seen in cattle ponds and near large cities in heavily polluted rivers.

Caiman skull (side view)

Caiman skull (top view)

Eye sockets

Crocodiles

In crocodiles, some teeth on the lower jaw stick out when the mouth is shut. Their spikelike teeth are perfect for gripping but not for chewing. Instead, for large prey, they seize part of the carcass in their jaws and roll over and over until a chunk tears away.

Crocodile skull (side view)

Prominent tooth

Crocodile skull (top view)

Lower jaw opening

Alligator skull (side view)

Alligators

Alligators are massive creatures, reaching up to 20 ft (6 m) in length. The American alligator can use its jaws with surprising delicacy—the female sometimes helps her eggs hatch by rolling them against the roof of her mouth with her tongue to gently crack them open.

Alligator skull (top view)

External nostrils

Tuatara

The tuatara is described as a "living fossil" because it is the sole survivor of an extinct group of animals. Its closest relatives died out millions of years ago, and no one knows why the tuatara alone survived. It is active at night and inhabits burrows, often shared with seabirds. It looks like a lizard, but it can function well in a cool climate. A lower internal temperature means its body is slow to convert food into energy, resulting in a very slow growth rate.

Males display this crest, called the nuchal crest, when trying to court a female.

Male tuatara

Five claws on feet

Tail can break off and drop when caught by a predator

Kith or kin?

These are the fossilized remains of *Homoeosaurus*, a tuataralike animal that lived about 140 million years ago in what is now Europe. During that time, sphenodontids, the group that contains the tuatara and *Homoeosaurus*, were widespread and successful animals. It seems likely that the sphenodontids separated from early lizards more than 200 million years ago.

Female tuatara

Tuataras can **live** up to **100 years.**

The name tuatara, a Māori word meaning "peaks on the back," refers to the crest that runs down the animal's back and tail.

A helping hand

Tuatara (above right) live alongside seabirds such as petrels and shearwaters (above left) and sometimes share their burrows with them. The birds cover the area in droppings, which attract insects, including beetles and crickets—the tuatara's favorite food. However, the tuatara may also eat the nestling birds.

Growing old together

Male tuatara grow to a length of about 2 ft (61 cm), while females are slightly shorter. Tuatara reach sexual maturity at about 20 years of age. The males have no external sexual organs, and mating takes place through the pair rubbing their cloacas (an opening for excretion) together. After mating, the female stores the sperm for a year, then lays between five and 15 eggs in a shallow burrow. The eggs hatch after 15 months.

SKULL STRUCTURE

The tuatara's skull has two bony arches that frame the back, similar to a crocodilian's. In most lizards, the lower arch is missing, while in snakes and many burrowing lizards, both arches are gone.

Bony arches

Serrated teeth are part of the jawbone

Saving the tuatara

Tuatara mostly live on small islands off the coast of New Zealand, free from predators. But rising sea levels due to climate change are threatening their home. To combat this, some conservationists are thinking of relocating these reptiles to the mainland. However, others argue that the presence of predators on the mainland can further reduce tuatara numbers. The tuatara may also affect the ecosystems and food chains on the mainland in unpredictable ways.

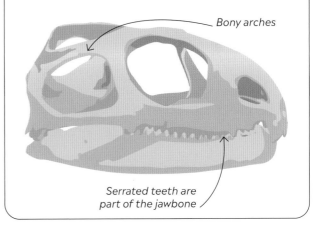

A bite to eat

Slow and steady

Tortoises or turtles do not have the speed or agility to catch fast-moving prey. Most feed on plants or slow-moving animals such as mollusks, worms, and insect larvae. They make the most of food that is nearby. The spur-thighed tortoise (above) also nibbles on any dead animal it finds.

Most reptiles are meat-eaters. Crocodiles and snakes are all carnivores, but some snakes have specialized diets and eat only birds' eggs (see pp.44–45) or fish eggs (eaten by sea snakes). Many lizards feed on insects, mammals, birds, and other reptiles, but large iguanas, some big skinks, and a few agamids are mostly vegetarian. Tortoises eat a variety of plants and occasionally eat meat. Freshwater turtles often eat worms, snails, and fish. Sea turtles feed on jellyfish, crabs, mollusks, and fish, but also eat plants.

Hook meets his end

In J. M. Barrie's *Peter Pan*, Captain Hook is haunted by the crocodile who ate his hand and wants more. Usually warned of its presence by a ticking clock in its stomach, Hook is finally tricked and eaten by the crocodile.

Crocodile larder

Nile crocodiles may share a large animal carcass (above). Crocodile stomachs are basketball-sized, so they cannot eat a big animal all at once. Prey is often left in one spot for finishing later. This led to the belief that crocodiles like to eat rotten meat, when in fact they prefer fresh meat.

Armlets

Stones

Bangles

Porcupine quills

Pieces of turtle shell

Stomach store

Crocodiles often devour hard, heavy objects such as stones and pieces of metal (left) and animal parts such as porcupine quills and turtle shell (above). The objects may be eaten to help the crocodile grind and digest its food.

DEVELOPING TEETH

Mammals have two sets of teeth—baby "milk" teeth and an adult set. Crocodiles shed teeth throughout their lives, and new ones constantly replace old ones.

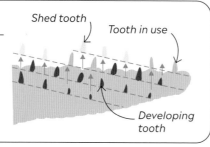

Shed tooth

Tooth in use

Developing tooth

The eyed lizard is mainly a ground dweller, but it is also an excellent climber.

Crickets and grasshoppers are the eyed lizard's favorite food.

Crispy cricket

After a rapid chase, the eyed lizard grabs a cricket with its jaws (above) and violently shakes it to stun it. The lizard passes the cricket to the back of its mouth and its jaw moves over the prey in a series of snapping movements. Its teeth grip and release the cricket as the jaw moves. The lizard must eat fast—the cricket may not be totally stunned and will try to escape. The majority of lizards are insect-eaters, and, in some areas, play an important role in keeping insect populations down.

Sharpshooters

With tongues longer than their bodies, chameleons are the sharpshooters of the lizard world. The tongue is hollow and unforked, with a large, sticky tip. A contracting muscle shoots it from the mouth at lightning speed with great accuracy to catch prey. Different muscles draw the tongue back into the mouth, where it is kept bunched up until it is needed again.

A tight squeeze

All snakes eat meat and have developed different ways of killing their food. Some kill their prey with venom. Pythons and boas, which mainly eat mammals, kill by constriction—by coiling their bodies around their prey and squeezing just enough to match the prey's breathing movements. This makes it hard for the prey to breathe, and it finally suffocates. Any mammal from a mouse to a deer can be prey, depending on the size of the snake.

Gigantic snake

One of the largest snakes to have ever existed was the *Titanoboa*, which lived in swamps and preyed on fish and other reptiles during the early Cenozoic Era (60–58 mya). Similar to modern-day boas, this giant constrictor killed its prey by suffocating and swallowing it.

2 Deadly embrace
The constricting snake tightens its grip until the rat's heart ceases beating. Only then will the snake release its hold. Death is fairly quick, and bones are rarely broken.

3 Big mouth
The snake's powerful, flexible jaws move easily (below)—upper and lower jaws move from side to side, and backward-pointing teeth grip tightly. As the jaws cover the rat's head, it looks like the snake is walking over its food.

OPEN WIDE

A special bone, like a double-jointed hinge, links a snake's upper jaw to the skull, while the lower jaw can be stretched sideways due to an elasticlike ligament. This jaw flexibility allows prey to be swallowed headfirst and whole, even when the prey is wider than the snake.

Jaw closed

Jaw open

Special hinged bone

4 Safety first
A small animal may disappear in just one or two gulps, but it can take an hour or more for larger prey. The snake's swallowing is mainly automatic—prey is drawn in by trunk muscles. But it can regurgitate food to escape any danger.

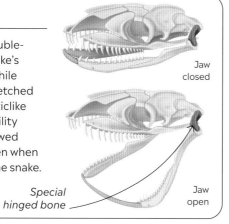

The snake's body can expand to make room for large prey.

5 Tight fit
Now, most of the rat has disappeared. The flexible, elasticlike ligament that connects the two halves of the snake's lower jaw allows it to open its mouth wide. As the lower jaws are forced apart, the muscle between them stretches to the shape of the prey.

Dinnertime

If prey walks by that might put up a dangerous fight, a snake can usually afford to ignore it—especially after a feast. A large constrictor might eat an entire leopard, but then may not eat again for up to a year.

1 Fangs of death

A boa constrictor usually swallows the head end of its prey first. If the prey is wriggly and fat, like this rat (right), the snake strikes with its long front teeth to secure the rat in its jaws before coiling round it.

Prey is swallowed headfirst so that it slips down the throat easily.

Snake eats snake

When a Californian kingsnake meets a rattlesnake, its jaws grip the rattler behind the head. It then loops its body around its prey, squeezing until the rattler suffocates.

It may take the snake days to digest this rat.

Despite its small canine teeth, the cheetah's jaw has a very tight grip.

Wild cat strike

A cheetah's massive jaws clamp on to the throat of its prey, such as an impala (right), causing it to suffocate. The prey dies either by strangulation or from the cheetah's sharp teeth and powerful claws.

When a
python constricts
its prey, it causes a
rapid death.

A cheetah carrying an impala

6 The end of the road

At this point, the snake could struggle to breathe, but it pushes its windpipe toward the front of its mouth and uses it as a "snorkel."

Venomous bite

Venomous snakes are found around the world, but the most lethal species live in tropical areas. Snakes inject venom (a type of toxin) into prey using special teeth or fangs. The most deadly snakes—such as sea snakes, vipers, and cobras—have fangs at the front of the upper jaw, while other snakes can have fangs at the back. A snake's venom can affect the nervous system, muscles, or blood of its victim. This helps the snake subdue prey so it can kill and eat it, or stun predators so the snake can flee.

Rattlesnakes

The extremely venomous rattlesnake is sometimes known as a pit viper due to the heat-sensitive pit between its nostrils and eyes. The pit enables the snake to locate the warm bodies of prey in the cool, dark night. A rattlesnake may shed its skin and add a new rattle two or three times a year (see p.25)—which disproves the myth that you can tell a snake's age by the number of rattles on its tail.

Cruel to be kind

Milking snakes for venom is still practiced in parts of the world, as venom is used to produce serum (fluid used in medicines to stop the effects of toxin) against snakebites. The snake, held by the head, is made to bite through tissue over a container. Gentle pressure on the venom sac in its cheeks then forces it to eject venom.

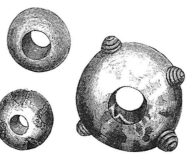

Snake stones

People once believed, wrongly, that snake stones could absorb venom and cure snake bites. These stones were made of burned bone, chalk, horn, or other absorbent materials.

Rapid vibrations of the rattle produce a sizzling sound.

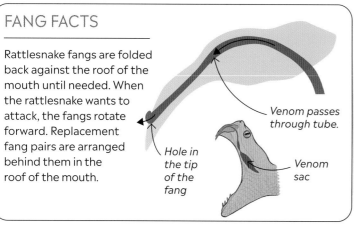

FANG FACTS

Rattlesnake fangs are folded back against the roof of the mouth until needed. When the rattlesnake wants to attack, the fangs rotate forward. Replacement fang pairs are arranged behind them in the roof of the mouth.

Venom passes through tube.

Hole in the tip of the fang

Venom sac

Killer shrew

The short-tailed shrew is one of the few mammals with a venomous bite. When it bites into prey—usually insects and earthworms—the venom in its saliva paralyzes its victim within seconds.

Venomous lizards

On land, there are two species of venomous lizards—the Gila monster and the Mexican beaded lizard. Both are found in the southwestern US and Mexico. Their venom comes from saliva glands in the lower jaw, which they chew into the victim.

Gila monster

Fishing for danger

Sea snakes include some of the world's most venomous species. Fishers in Asia are sometimes bitten while disentangling the snakes from their nets. Sea kraits, however, rarely bite—they are not aggressive.

Sea krait

Rattlesnakes have very sticky skin that helps hold onto water.

Star performers

Snakes have featured in literature for centuries. In *Antony and Cleopatra*, a play by English playwright William Shakespeare, the ancient Egyptian pharaoh Cleopatra is devastated when she gets news that her lover Antony is dead, and lets an asp (venomous Egyptian serpent) bite her so she can die, too.

Egg eaters

Some snakes only eat eggs, and over time their bodies have become specialized for this task. Small eggs, especially soft-shelled ones laid by lizards and some other snakes, are easy for a snake to split open with its teeth and eat. Larger, hard-shelled eggs, such as birds' eggs, need special treatment. True egg-eating snakes eat only birds' eggs, which they swallow whole, as they have few teeth. Toothlike spines along the snake's backbone crack open the egg as it moves down the throat.

Diet of eggs

In some parts of the world, birds only lay eggs at certain times of the year, so a snake may have to go a long time without food. Fortunately, an egg-eating snake can regurgitate (bring up) eggshell so that no space is wasted in its stomach. This means it can eat as many eggs as it finds and doesn't have to waste energy digesting the shell.

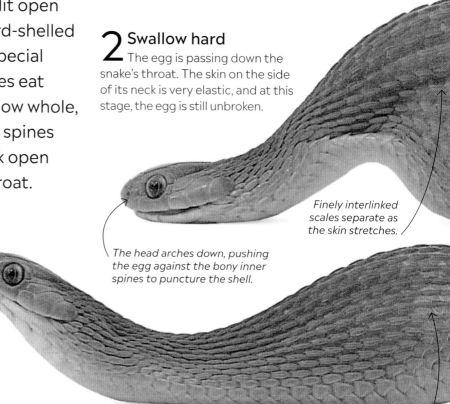

2 Swallow hard
The egg is passing down the snake's throat. The skin on the side of its neck is very elastic, and at this stage, the egg is still unbroken.

Finely interlinked scales separate as the skin stretches.

The head arches down, pushing the egg against the bony inner spines to puncture the shell.

The bulge is noticeably smaller.

3 Spiny bones
The passage of the egg has now been stopped by the toothlike spines on the underside of the neck bones.

A valve at the entrance of the stomach accepts yolks and liquids but rejects pieces of shell.

4 Going down
Once the egg is punctured, the snake's body muscles work in waves to squeeze out the contents, which continue on to the stomach. The snake then bends its body into S-shaped curves to force the eggshell back toward its mouth.

5 And up it comes
Depending on the size of the egg, it can take five minutes to an hour for it to be completely swallowed. Finally, the snake's mouth gapes wide and the compacted shell fragments are brought up, still held together by the sticky egg membranes.

The jagged edges of the shell pieces are stuck together. The contents of the egg have been drained.

Regurgitated shell

1 Too greedy?

An African egg-eater, with a lightly built skull and mouth lined with sticky ridges, is about to swallow an egg that is twice the width of its body.

Mouth ridges grip the egg as it passes into the snake's throat.

The egg is remarkably resistant to crushing thanks to its shape, but it is pierced by the snake's bony spines.

Danger!

Monitor lizards, some of which are giants of the reptile world, are experts at finding food. Many feed on the carcasses of dead animals and on live animals—but even a nest of eggs is not safe with them around.

Survival

Reptiles use many methods to frighten away enemies. Some reptiles inflate themselves with air, then blow it out with a hiss, while others use camouflage to avoid being seen in the first place. Several lizards and some snakes sacrifice their tail to escape a predator. Some American horned lizards swell up and squirt blood from tiny eye capillaries to intimidate enemies. The armadillo lizard from South Africa coils up into a tight ball to protect its soft belly—it has thick, spiny scales along its head, back, and tail that form a perfect shield.

On guard

The Australian frilled lizard has a "frill" of loose skin normally kept folded flat and attached to its neck. When startled by a predator, the lizard erects this rufflike collar, which can be four times the width of its body. If challenged, the lizard will also bob its head, lash its tail, and wave its legs. While most lizards under attack try to escape, the frilled lizard meets danger head on.

Stinky stinkpot

The stinkpot or common musk turtle (right), which is both smelly and aggressive, gives off a stink when cornered by a predator. Its stink is produced by a pair of glands in the soft skin of the thighs.

Stinkpot

Playing dead

When all else fails, some snakes will pretend to be dead. When the European grass snake (right) meets an enemy, it puffs and hisses loudly. If this does not scare off the attacker, the snake rolls over onto its back, wriggles, then lies still with its mouth wide open and tongue hanging out. Even if the snake is turned over, it will stay "dead" and not move so as to not give the game away.

Frill fully erected to scare aggressors

Its gaping mouth expands the neck frill. The wider the mouth is opened, the more erect the frill becomes.

Survival gear

To survive adverse conditions, humans use special clothes and equipment. Reptiles cannot survive extreme temperatures, but they can adapt to changing weather within their environment.

The tale of a tail

When grabbed by the tail, most lizards will shed it to avoid death. Several lizards waggle their tail when first attacked, which helps confuse the predator. The vertebrae, or small backbones along the tail (below), have special cracks where the tail can break off. When an enemy grasps the tail, the muscles, which are also arranged for separating, contract and cause a vertebra to break off.

Fracture points along the tail

Tail has been recently shed

1 Breaking free

This tree skink gave up its tail to a predator. The separated tail-part often twitches for several minutes after shedding, confusing the attacker so the lizard can escape.

The new tail looks the same on the outside but has a simple tube of cartilage instead of vertebrae on the inside.

2 Growing stronger

In two months, a new tail-part becomes visible. However, the new tail doesn't replace the stored energy that was in the original tail, which was built up for a time when food may be scarce. It is therefore not surprising that some species live longer when they have a complete tail.

Fully regrown tail

3 New for old

After eight months, the tail has almost fully regrown. It can be broken off again, but only in the old part, where there are vertebrae. Growing a new tail uses a lot of the skink's stored energy.

Blending **in**

Many reptiles blend in with their surroundings. This is known as camouflage, and it helps reptiles avoid being spotted by both prey and predators. In some reptiles, their skin colors match their surroundings, and in others, their skin pattern helps hide the body's outline. In a few reptiles, physical features improve camouflage—such as the side fringes and leaf-shaped tails of tree-living geckos.

Hiding in the open

The omnivorous, large-bodied Mary River turtle is found only in Queensland, Australia. It has a brownish shell covered with algae, which helps it easily hide from predators in open waters.

A chameleon's skin is made up of several layers of color cells. One type of cell, called a melanophore, allows the chameleon to change color.

Pigments moving to and from the skin's surface in the melanophores causes the color to change.

The chameleon has changed color to match its surroundings.

Master of camouflage

Lizards, especially chameleons (above), are the masters of camouflage. Many can lighten or darken the color of their skins as needed. Although these changes take place so that the chameleon can match its environment, other factors like light level, temperature of its surroundings, and its mood can affect the color a chameleon takes on.

Waiting for a meal

Lying still in the leaf litter of tropical African forests, the Gaboon viper is nearly invisible in the dappled light and shade as it lies in wait for rodents, frogs, and birds. Although unaggressive and unlikely to attack humans, its bite would be dangerously venomous to anyone who had the bad luck to tread on it. In fact, the fangs of the Gaboon viper are the longest of any snake—up to 2 in (50 mm) long.

Outside its leafy environment, the Gaboon viper can easily be spotted due to its vivid markings.

Rocky danger

The black caiman is often mistaken for rocks as it lies in muddy water. Staying unseen gives it an advantage when hunting for food.

Leaf green

This little tree skink (above) is hard to spot against the palm trees it lives on in Indonesia, the Philippines, and the Solomon Islands. Its bright-green and mottled-brown body makes it almost invisible.

Lots of legs

Legs and feet are vital for many reptiles, although snakes and some lizards do well without them. Legs and feet are adapted to a reptile's habitat. Desert lizards often have long scales fringing their toes, which help them walk on soft sand. Webbed feet, or paddle-shaped limbs, help aquatic turtles swim. In other swimming reptiles, such as crocodiles, the tail propels them forward and the limbs are folded back out of the way.

The hare and the tortoise

In the famous fable by Aesop, the hare is so confident of winning his race with the slow and ponderous tortoise that he falls asleep by the wayside, and the tortoise crosses the finish line first. It is certainly true that although tortoises are slow, they make steady progress and can travel pretty long distances, seldom stopping for a rest.

Legs of all sorts

A reptile's feet reflect its lifestyle. The slightly webbed back feet of caimans help propel them through the water. The powerful legs and feet of plated and monitor lizards are good for digging. The sharp-clawed toes of girdled lizards help them grip flaking rock surfaces. But in some of the smaller skinks, the tiny limbs barely support the animal.

Caiman

Plated lizard

Monitor lizard

East African girdled lizard

Blue-tongued skink

All five toes spread out to achieve maximum grip.

50

Geckos have no trouble moving vertically or hanging horizontally.

Underside of the tokay gecko

Get a grip

The tokay gecko (above, left, and right) is a fairly large gecko from east Asia. It is one of the best lizard climbers and can scale a wall, run across a ceiling, and even cling to a pane of glass. It grips by using pads on the ends of its fingers and toes. These pads are covered with thousands of microscopic hairlike structures that allow it to cling to almost any surface it walks on.

Loss of legs

This glass lizard (left) is often mistaken for a snake. It has no front legs and only tiny remnants of back legs. Many lizards, particularly burrowing types, have evolved in the same way as snakes—their long body without legs is better equipped for a life underground. Some, such as the glass lizard, live above ground in rocky habitats or thick vegetation.

Elongated body resembles that of a snake.

LITTLE LIMBS

In most snakes, all traces of limbs have been lost. In some of the more primitive groups, such as boas and pythons, tiny remnants of hip bones and hind limbs remain. These appear as small "claws" at the tail base, on either side of the vent, or the anal opening.

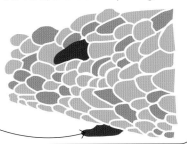

Vestigial limbs (small remnants of hind legs) are of no use in movement, but the male may use them to stimulate the female.

Geckos have a **sticky pad** on the **end** of the **tail** to help **grip.**

Tokay gecko, climbing

Ground control

Most lizards rely on swiftness and agility to hunt and run from predators. Their legs and feet are specially adapted to where they live. Turtles have powerful legs that carry their heavy, protective shell and propel them forward steadily. Snakes move in a variety of ways, depending on their surroundings. Crocodilians are most at home in water. On land, they crawl, dragging their bellies along the ground, but some smaller crocodilians can gallop when they want to move rapidly.

Palm flexed against the ground

Back legs provide most of the thrust.

Three feet are kept on the ground, and only one foot moves when the lizard is advancing at a slow pace.

Moving foot

Tegu lizard

3 Two at a time
When a lizard trots, the body is supported by two legs at a time (the diagonal pairs). At times, both front feet and one hind foot are taken off the ground.

Two legs are better than four
If disturbed when on the ground, the crested water dragon (right) from Asia may rear up on its hind legs and run while upright. Several lizards use this type of bipedal (two-legged) movement as they are able to run much faster on two legs than four.

Long tail helps lizard balance when running on its hind legs.

High-speed sprinter
The six-lined racerunner lizard, found in North America, is one of the fastest reptiles on land. It can reach a speed of 11 mph (18 kph).

Lizard locomotion

A majority of lizards have four legs with five toes each. In most lizards, the back legs are stronger than the front and power the animal forward. Lizards that live underground, however, often have much smaller legs or even none at all—they glide and wind through burrows, similar to snakes.

1 Palm power
When this tegu lizard moves, its front claws point forward, palm down. The animal's forward thrust comes from the flexed palm pushing against the ground.

2 Side to side
A lizard increases its stride by bending its body from side to side. The order in which the limbs move depends on how fast the lizard is traveling.

One of the world's fastest snakes, the black mamba can move at speeds of up to 9 mph (15 kph).

Alert crested water dragon, standing on all four feet

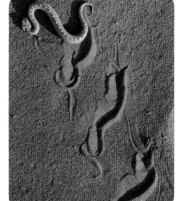

Sidewinding

Now you see me
Snakes move in four ways. A sidewinding Namib desert adder (right) is leaving these tracks in the sand. The snake lifts loops of its body clear of the sand as it moves sideways. Sidewinding stops the snake from slipping when it moves across a soft sand dune.

SNAKE MOVEMENT

Besides sidewinding, snakes may use three other methods to move: serpentine motion, concertina motion, and rectilinear motion.

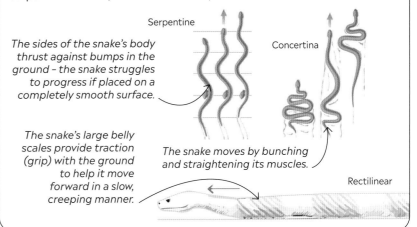

Serpentine

The sides of the snake's body thrust against bumps in the ground – the snake struggles to progress if placed on a completely smooth surface.

Concertina

The snake's large belly scales provide traction (grip) with the ground to help it move forward in a slow, creeping manner.

The snake moves by bunching and straightening its muscles.

Rectilinear

Highly strung

This rear-fanged mangrove snake lies high in a tree until late afternoon, when it raids birds' nests for food.

Mangrove snake

Furry flier

Flying squirrels glide using folds of skin between their limbs, like some reptiles. If the squirrels eat too much, they can't fly.

Life in **trees**

Arboreal (tree-dwelling) lizards are well adapted to their habitat. Many have well-developed claws for gripping tree trunks, or special toe pads (see p.51) for clinging to smooth leaf surfaces, and long tails that twist around branches to help them balance. Some tree snakes have ridges on their belly scales for extra grip. Many arboreal reptiles live on the Pacific Islands, to which their ancestors most likely traveled on floating vegetation.

Clingy coils

This tree boa from South America has a stretchy body and strong tail, which help it climb trees. It reaches up and coils around a branch, hauling up the rest of its body as it goes.

Tree boa

Flying gecko

Flying ace

This flying gecko (left) has webbed feet and skin folds along its sides, legs, and tail. These act as a parachute when the lizard glides through the air to escape trouble or to swoop on food. Its color and texture act as camouflage against tree bark.

Cooling down

The trinket snake from India is a part-time tree-dweller. In hot weather, it shelters in termite mounds or under rocks on the ground. In cooler weather, it moves up into trees and bushes.

Trinket snake

Hanging on

An emerald tree boa catches a bird (left) while coiled around a branch to support itself.

Garden lizard

Bloodsucker

The garden lizard has a long, slender tail and a body like a chameleon's. It changes color rapidly—especially its head, which may turn red. The lips of some garden lizards turn so red that they are nicknamed "bloodsuckers."

Daredevil dragons

A flying dragon parachutes through the air using flaps of skin stretched over elongated ribs. These "wings" fold back when not in use.

Day gecko

Day duty

Most geckos are good climbers because their toes' friction pads help them grip different surfaces. They are mostly nocturnal and eat insects and fruit, but some, such as the day gecko, are active during the day and eat palm flowers' nectar.

Flying dragon

55

Waterproofed

Reptiles are mainly land animals, but some live in water. Crocodilians, a few lizards, some snakes, and terrapins and turtles all spend much of their lives submerged. Most reptiles lay their eggs on dry land—or the eggs would drown—but some sea snakes found in Asia, northern Australia, and the Pacific Islands give birth to live young that can swim and come up for air. Different reptiles use their watery home differently—crocodilians use it to swim, hunt, and cool off, while marine iguanas feed on its algae.

Snorkel snout

In calm water, an alligator can rest, submerged, with just its nose disc above the surface. When it dives, its special muscles and flaps close over the ears and nostrils. Well-developed eyelids protect the eyes, and a flap of transparent skin covers them, allowing it to see underwater.

Tail walking

If a crocodile is being chased, or if it is giving chase, it can move very fast, even leaping out of the water. This "tail walk" (left) demonstrates how graceful and at ease the animal is in water.

Eyes are high on the head.

A caiman lies still in the water to go unnoticed.

Monsters of the deep

Myths of strange creatures living in deep waters, such as in Scotland's Loch Ness, have been around for centuries. People spotting aquatic reptiles in the water probably sparked these myths.

Did you ever meet—

Soft backs

Water turtles tend to have streamlined shells that are suited to swimming. Soft-shelled turtles (left) have the flattest shells—perfect for hiding beneath sand and mud on the riverbed. Their feet have long, webbed toes that give them extra thrust when moving through water.

Walking on water

When frightened, the basilisk lizard (above and left) drops onto water. Broad soles and fringed scales on its feet enable it to scuttle across the water's surface on its back legs. As the lizard loses speed, it sinks and swims to safety.

Nostrils lie just above water level.

The shell is covered with horny plates called scutes.

Underwater breathing

All turtles have lungs, but species that are aquatic can also breathe through their skin and throat lining. Some can tolerate very low oxygen levels and survive for weeks underwater, but the red-eared terrapin (above) can only last for two to three hours.

Water baby

This young caiman is well adapted to life in water. Its eyes, nostrils, and ears are high on its head so that it can breathe and see, while the rest of its body lies hidden underwater. This is an advantage when hunting prey that comes to the water's edge to drink. Tucking its legs and webbed feet against its sides, it can propel itself forward in the water with its powerful tail. The caiman depends on water—if it lies in the hot sunshine for long periods without cooling off, it will die.

Crocodiles can **hold** their **breath underwater** for more than **an hour.**

Natural enemies

Reptiles have a number of enemies. Large birds, such as owls and eagles, and some mammals, such as hedgehogs and cats, all prey on snakes and lizards. Some reptiles, such as the Asian king cobra and monitor lizards, eat their own kind. But reptiles' greatest enemies are humans. Crocodiles, snakes, and lizards are killed for their skins, and snakes are captured so their venom can be used for medical research.

Easily outmatched

A jaguar often turns a caiman—a dangerous predator to most other animals—into its prey. Even if the caiman tries to escape, the jaguar—an excellent swimmer—will be able to pursue it. A jaguar also has the strongest bite force of all the big cats, allowing it to overpower the caiman easily.

Rikki-Tikki-Tavi

In 1894, British author Rudyard Kipling wrote *The Jungle Book*, and created a hero out of a little mongoose, Rikki-Tikki-Tavi. This mammal became the protector of a British family in colonial India, first killing a lethal krait snake, then a cobra (left).

Indian cobra

When the cobra's hood is extended, the "eye" is meant to frighten aggressors.

The cobra's body is bunched, ready for attack.

Hood spread in attack

Enemy number one

One of the most famous enemies of many snakes, particularly of cobras (left), is the mongoose (above right). In any fight, it is likely to win, relying on its speed and agility to avoid the venomous snake's lunges. The mongoose will dart in and bite the back of the snake's neck, or grab the back of the snake's head until the snake gives up the struggle. Mongooses were introduced into the Caribbean islands to reduce snake numbers but became bigger pests themselves, attacking small animals and poultry.

Stiff hairs on the back of the mongoose are raised as added protection.

Mongoose

The mongoose's body is lightly poised on its back paws so that it can move quickly, if needed.

Feet first

The secretary bird (left) stamps its feet and flaps its wings to disturb prey. When a snake shows itself, the bird kicks or stamps on it while covering the snake with its wings to stop it from moving into a position to defend itself. If stamping does not work, then the bird carries the snake high into the air and drops it.

Kaliya's wives begged Krishna to forgive the serpent.

👁 EYEWITNESS

Harvey Tweats and Tom Whitehurst
During the COVID-19 pandemic, British teenagers Tom Whitehurst (left) and Harvey Tweats (right) started Celtic Reptile & Amphibian—an organization that aims to rewild the UK and restore native reptile and amphibian species that have been extinct in the country for centuries. Whitehurst and Tweats have also opened the UK's largest breeding center for reptiles and amphibians.

Krishna defeats Kaliya

In one tale from Hindu mythology, Krishna (a human form of the God Vishnu) danced on the many heads of the ferocious serpent Kaliya (above) to crush it. Kaliya had threatened the people of a village, but Krishna saved them.

Just good friends

Because the majority of reptiles are meat-eaters, their relationship with other animals is usually that of predator and prey. But sometimes they have symbiotic relationships, where two different species depend on each other in a common habitat. A number of reptiles live in peace with other animals. Lizards and snakes sometimes use the same termite mound to incubate their eggs. Tortoises and lizards have been known to share a burrow with opossums, racoons, rabbits, and rats. Even rattlesnakes can live peacefully with others in such a home.

A friend indeed

African helmeted turtles clean tiny parasites from hippopotamuses (left) and rhinoceroses. Some turtles pull algae from other turtles' shells using their jaws—and then swap places.

Three's not a crowd

All sorts of reptiles end up living side by side for different reasons. The hinge-back tortoise (right) hides in its burrow from the hot African sunshine, waiting for rain. The house snake (below) searches the same hole for rats and mice to eat, while the skink (far right) may be hiding from a predator.

Cleaning up

Outside of the reptile world, there are many animals that help other animals—helping themselves in the process. These small cleaner fish (below) pick unwanted parasites from the large fish's skin. At the same time, they're getting a meal of food fragments that cling to the bigger fish.

Marine hitchhikers

Sometimes the relationship between two creatures that share the same environment only benefits one of them. Remora, a type of marine fish, often attach themselves to a sea turtle (above) to catch a ride on its shell. They also occasionally hide under it to avoid capture. While mostly patient, the turtle may push them away when the remora try to snatch its food.

An easy meal

Galápagos lava lizards can be found close to the nesting sites of marine iguanas. The large herbivorous iguanas often attract swarms of flies as they bask in the sunshine, and rely on the smaller lava lizards to pick off the pesky insects.

Good partners

Birds may sometimes pluck scraps of food and parasites from the gaping mouths of crocodiles (above). Some birds, such as the water dikkop, nest near crocodiles. This benefits both animals—predators will hesitate to attack the birds with crocodiles nearby, and the birds' reaction to an approaching enemy warns the crocodiles.

Clean up

Building for tourism has caused the loss of many nesting sites for sea turtles around the world. Today, Lamma Island in Hong Kong, China, is the only regular nesting site for green sea turtles in the South China Sea. Many conservation organizations are taking action to clean up beaches on Lamma Island and preserve their habitat before the turtle population in the area dies out permanently.

An eye to
the future

Unless we reduce our impact on Earth's ecological systems, many reptiles may face extinction. Over 150 million years, a wide variety of reptiles has declined to just four groups, and they now face a greater threat than ever before—destruction of their habitats by humans. Today, people and governments are more aware, and they are working to conserve more and more species.

Big head

The head of this aptly named big-headed turtle (below) is so large that it cannot be drawn into its shell. Found in Southeast Asia, the turtle spends its days buried in gravel or under rocks in cool mountain streams. Due to its unique appearance, it is often captured and sold as a pet or killed by humans to make souvenirs.

Snakeskin boots

Dirty dealing

While many conservationists around the world are working to save reptiles, several species are still being slaughtered for their skin. However, leather goods made from plastic and plant-based materials are becoming more and more popular, replacing leather skins.

Around 21 percent of reptile species are facing extinction.

While it is mainly a ground-dweller, this snake often climbs trees to feed on prey.

Unhappy pet

The Pacific ground boa (right) lives in a variety of habitats—forests, farms, and near human dwellings—on the Solomon Islands. The main danger to its existence is the loss of its habitat. It is sometimes kept as a pet, but often refuses to eat and dies in captivity.

Safe—for how long?

Although still fairly common, the giant skink of the Solomon Islands faces a problem shared by many other reptiles—its habitat is rapidly being taken over by humans. There is concern that these lizards will soon face extinction with the decline of their home and food source. Giant skinks are also sold as exotic pets, further reducing their numbers in the wild.

Down the ladder

Snake species are rapidly declining. If something is not done to help them, the only remaining evidence of these animals will be in pictures, models, and board games.

👁 EYEWITNESS

Romulus Whitaker

In the 1970s, American-Indian conservationist Romulus Whitaker set up the Chennai Snake Park, India's first reptile park, and the Madras Crocodile Bank research station. He has studied the king cobra and its habitat and worked hard at conserving Indian gharials. Whitaker was awarded the Padma Shri (India's fourth-highest civilian award) in 2018.

Reptile classification

Almost 12,000 species of reptiles are currently known to us. Like all living things, reptile species are classified and given a two-part scientific name. Reptiles are an animal class that is divided into four orders: turtles and tortoises, crocodilians, tuatara, and snakes and lizards.

Upper and lower eyelids are joined to form turretlike eyes.

Jackson's chameleon, *Trioceros jacksonii*

Extendable tongue is many times the length of its jaw.

Sticky, club-shaped tip traps insects.

Classifying reptiles

Jackson's chameleon, from East Africa, is also known as the three-horned chameleon. Its scientific name, given by zoologist George Boulenger in 1896, is *Trioceros jacksonii*. It has a flattened body, feet divided into two groups of toes, and a prehensile tail. Its eyes are housed in movable, turret-shaped structures. These features point to the fact that it belongs to the chameleon family of reptiles, within the order that includes lizards.

Saddle-shaped markings on back

Boa constrictor, *Boa constrictor*, coiled on a branch

Classification levels

In scientific classification, species are arranged in groups of increasing size. The boa constrictor is classified as the species *constrictor*, one of the four species under the genus *Boa*, which is in the Boidae family. Boidae is in the suborder Serpentes (which contains all snakes) and is part of the order Squamata (which includes snakes and lizards). Squamata is in the class Reptilia, which is in the phylum Chordata (and includes all animals with backbones).

Color varies across different parts of the snake's body.

SPECIES	*constrictor*
GENUS	*Boa*
FAMILY	Boidae
SUBORDER	Serpentes
ORDER	Squamata
CLASS	Reptilia
PHYLUM	Chordata

Nano-chameleon, *Brookesia nana*

New discoveries

Every year, new reptiles are discovered as scientists probe remote habitats and reexamine known species. Recent discoveries include a new species of Papuan ground snake from Papua New Guinea, found in 2021. In the same year, the world's smallest reptile, a nano-chameleon, was found in Madagascar—this chameleon is so tiny that it measures 0.9 in (22 mm) in length, including its tail!

TURTLES AND TORTOISES

Reptiles in this order have a hard or rubbery shell enclosing soft parts of the body. They live on land as well as in water and cut up their food with sharp-edged jaws.

Order: Testudines

Families: 14

Species: 363

Spotted turtle,
Clemmys guttata

TUATARA

Found only in New Zealand, tuatara resemble lizards but have a different skull structure and quite different ancestry. They grow slowly but can live to a great age.

Order: Rhynchocephalia

Families: 1

Species: 1

Tuatara,
Sphenodon punctatus

CROCODILIANS

Semiaquatic predators, crocodilians have long bodies, powerful jaws, and eyes and nostrils positioned high on their heads. Their backs are protected by large, bony scales.

Order: Crocodylia

Families: 3

Species: 27

Nile crocodile,
Crocodylus niloticus

SNAKES AND LIZARDS

Order: Squamata

Suborders: 3

Egyptian cobra,
Naja haje

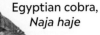

Snakes
These legless predators have cylindrical bodies and gaping jaws. Some kill by constricting their prey, while others bite with venomous fangs.

Suborder: Serpentes

Families: 30

Species: 4,038

Lizards
The most varied group of reptiles, lizards typically have four well-developed legs and keen senses. Often fast-moving, some shed their tails if attacked.

Suborder: Lacertilia

Families: 37

Species: 7,511

Rainbow agama,
Agama agama

Amphisbaenians
This group contains wormlike reptiles with cylindrical bodies and rings of scales. Suited for life underground, they are rarely seen above ground except after rain.

Suborder: Amphisbaena

Families: 6

Species: 201

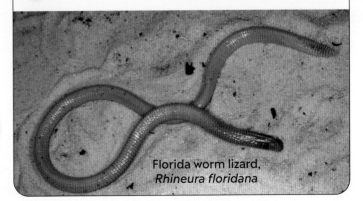

Florida worm lizard,
Rhineura floridana

Reptile evolution

Reptiles first appeared on Earth more than 300 million years ago (mya), in the Carboniferous Period. They evolved into distinct groups, and by the Jurassic Period, they were the world's dominant animals—until an asteroid probably wiped out the nonbird dinosaurs and many other reptiles around 66 mya. Today, five evolutionary lines remain, including the direct descendants of dinosaurs—birds.

Fossil skeleton of *Edmontosaurus*

Evidence from the past

Fossils play a key part in showing how reptiles have evolved. This skeleton (right) belongs to *Edmontosaurus*, a dinosaur that lived in the late Cretaceous Period, around 66 mya.

GEOLOGICAL PERIODS

CARBONIFEROUS	PERMIAN	TRIASSIC	JURASSIC	CRETACEOUS	CENOZOIC
359	299	252	201	145	66	0

MILLION YEARS AGO

Turtles and tortoises

Chelonians (turtles and tortoises) may have evolved from early anapsids, although chelonians' ancestry is uncertain. Prehistoric kinds included giant sea turtles.

Red-bellied turtle, *Pseudemys rubriventris*

Extinct anapsids

The anapsids were one of the first kinds of reptile to evolve. Many of them—including *Procolophon*—are thought to have fed on plants.

Skull of *Procolophon*

ANAPSIDS

Mosasaurs

Related to lizards, mosasaurs were large marine predators with biting or crushing teeth, webbed feet, and paddlelike tails. They evolved in the Cretaceous Period, spent their entire lives at sea, and gave birth to live young.

Jaw fossil of a mosasaur

Snakes and lizards

The first fossil lizards date back more than 200 million years. Snakes are more recent and evolved from lizards. Some snakes still have traces of hind limbs, showing that their ancestors moved on legs.

LEPIDOSAURS

Basilisk lizard, *Basiliscus basiliscus*

Tuatara, *Sphenodon punctatus*

REPTILE EVOLUTION

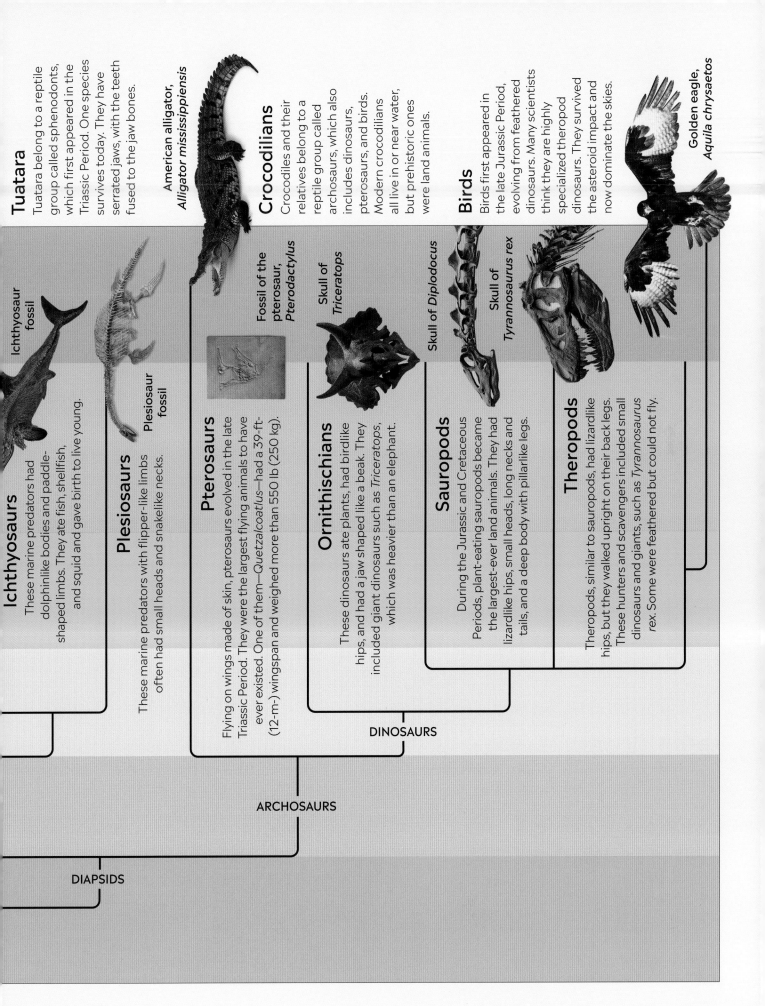

Tuatara

Tuatara belong to a reptile group called sphenodonts, which first appeared in the Triassic Period. One species survives today. They have serrated jaws, with the teeth fused to the jaw bones.

American alligator, *Alligator mississippiensis*

Crocodilians

Crocodiles and their relatives belong to a reptile group called archosaurs, which also includes dinosaurs, pterosaurs, and birds. Modern crocodilians all live in or near water, but prehistoric ones were land animals.

Birds

Birds first appeared in the late Jurassic Period, evolving from feathered dinosaurs. Many scientists think they are highly specialized theropod dinosaurs. They survived the asteroid impact and now dominate the skies.

Golden eagle, *Aquila chrysaetos*

Ichthyosaur fossil

Ichthyosaurs

These marine predators had dolphinlike bodies and paddle-shaped limbs. They ate fish, shellfish, and squid and gave birth to live young.

Plesiosaur fossil

Plesiosaurs

These marine predators with flipper-like limbs often had small heads and snakelike necks.

Fossil of the pterosaur, *Pterodactylus*

Pterosaurs

Flying on wings made of skin, pterosaurs evolved in the late Triassic Period. They were the largest flying animals to have ever existed. One of them—*Quetzalcoatlus*—had a 39-ft- (12-m-) wingspan and weighed more than 550 lb (250 kg).

Skull of *Triceratops*

Ornithischians

These dinosaurs ate plants, had birdlike hips, and had a jaw shaped like a beak. They included giant dinosaurs such as *Triceratops*, which was heavier than an elephant.

Skull of *Diplodocus*

Sauropods

During the Jurassic and Cretaceous Periods, plant-eating sauropods became the largest-ever land animals. They had lizardlike hips, small heads, long necks and tails, and a deep body with pillarlike legs.

Skull of *Tyrannosaurus rex*

Theropods

Theropods, similar to sauropods, had lizardlike hips, but they walked upright on their back legs. These hunters and scavengers included small dinosaurs and giants, such as *Tyrannosaurus rex*. Some were feathered but could not fly.

DINOSAURS

ARCHOSAURS

DIAPSIDS

Threats

Over 20 percent of reptiles are threatened with extinction. They face many threats, including hunting and habitat loss, which is especially harmful for reptiles who only live on certain islands and have nowhere else to go.

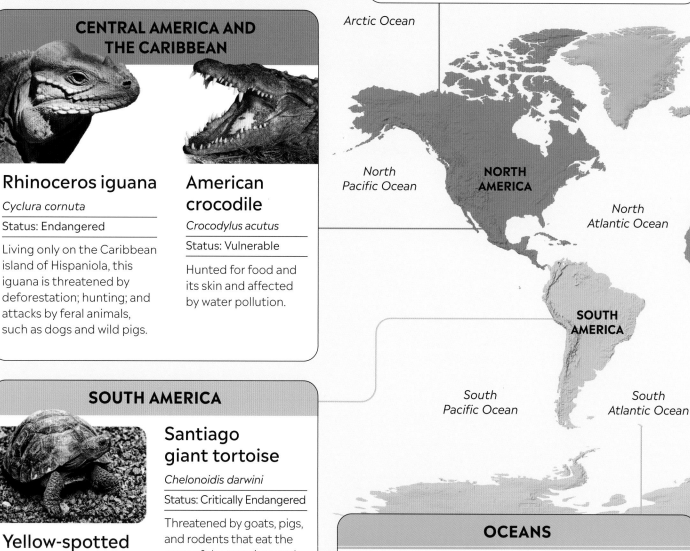

NORTH AMERICA

Wood turtle

Glyptemys insculpta

Status: Endangered

Impacted by road traffic and habitat change.

Alligator snapping turtle

Macrochelys temminckii

Status: Vulnerable

Threats include drainage of its watery habitat and hunting for its meat and shell.

CENTRAL AMERICA AND THE CARIBBEAN

Rhinoceros iguana

Cyclura cornuta

Status: Endangered

Living only on the Caribbean island of Hispaniola, this iguana is threatened by deforestation; hunting; and attacks by feral animals, such as dogs and wild pigs.

American crocodile

Crocodylus acutus

Status: Vulnerable

Hunted for food and its skin and affected by water pollution.

SOUTH AMERICA

Yellow-spotted river turtle

Podocnemis unifilis

Status: Vulnerable

Vulnerable to hunting for its eggs and meat and to capture for the pet trade.

Santiago giant tortoise

Chelonoidis darwini

Status: Critically Endangered

Threatened by goats, pigs, and rodents that eat the eggs of the tortoises and destroy their habitat.

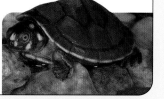

OCEANS

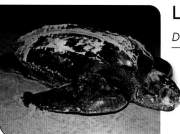

Leatherback turtle

Dermochelys coriacea

Status: Vulnerable

Threats include collisions with ships, fishing, and plastic waste in the oceans.

Arctic Ocean

North Pacific Ocean

NORTH AMERICA

North Atlantic Ocean

SOUTH AMERICA

South Pacific Ocean

South Atlantic Ocean

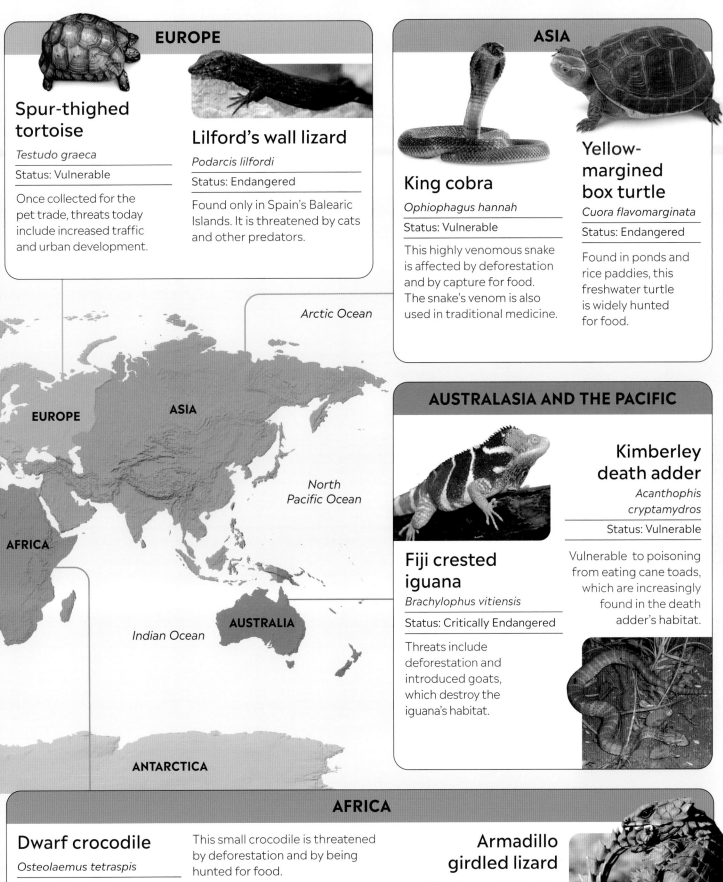

EUROPE

Spur-thighed tortoise

Testudo graeca

Status: Vulnerable

Once collected for the pet trade, threats today include increased traffic and urban development.

Lilford's wall lizard

Podarcis lilfordi

Status: Endangered

Found only in Spain's Balearic Islands. It is threatened by cats and other predators.

ASIA

King cobra

Ophiophagus hannah

Status: Vulnerable

This highly venomous snake is affected by deforestation and by capture for food. The snake's venom is also used in traditional medicine.

Yellow-margined box turtle

Cuora flavomarginata

Status: Endangered

Found in ponds and rice paddies, this freshwater turtle is widely hunted for food.

Arctic Ocean

EUROPE

ASIA

North Pacific Ocean

AFRICA

Indian Ocean

AUSTRALIA

ANTARCTICA

AUSTRALASIA AND THE PACIFIC

Fiji crested iguana

Brachylophus vitiensis

Status: Critically Endangered

Threats include deforestation and introduced goats, which destroy the iguana's habitat.

Kimberley death adder

Acanthophis cryptamydros

Status: Vulnerable

Vulnerable to poisoning from eating cane toads, which are increasingly found in the death adder's habitat.

AFRICA

Dwarf crocodile

Osteolaemus tetraspis

Status: Vulnerable

This small crocodile is threatened by deforestation and by being hunted for food.

Armadillo girdled lizard

Ouroborus cataphractus

Status: Near Threatened

Threats include the illegal pet trade.

Glossary

Boa constrictor

AMNION
A membrane that surrounds and protects a developing animal before it hatches or before it is born.

AMPHIBIAN
One of a group of cold-blooded vertebrates (backboned animals). They have moist skin and mostly lay eggs in water.

ANTIVENOM
A substance used to counter the effects of a snakebite. It is made from snake venom.

BASK
To warm up by lying in sunshine. Reptiles bask to adjust their body temperature.

BINOCULAR VISION
Vision in which both eyes face forward, letting an animal see in 3D. Humans and some reptiles have binocular vision.

BIPEDAL
Walking on two legs instead of four.

CAMOUFLAGE
The process of an animal disguising itself by blending in with its natural surroundings.

CARAPACE
The domed shell of a chelonian, made of hard scales, or scutes, over plates of bone.

CARNIVORE
Any animal that eats other animals.

CARTILAGE
A tough, flexible substance between bones, letting them slide over each other at joints.

CHELONIANS
Reptile group that includes tortoises and turtles and has a bony or leathery shell.

CLASSIFICATION
A system of identifying living beings and showing how they are linked through evolution.

Carapace

COLD-BLOODED
An animal that uses the Sun's heat to keep warm. Most living reptiles are cold-blooded.

COLUBRIDAE
The largest family of snakes, containing more than 2,000 species. The snakes in this family are called colubrids.

CONSTRICTION
Suffocating prey by slowly squeezing it to death.

CROCODYLOMORPHS
An animal group that includes crocodiles and all their extinct relatives.

EGG TOOTH
A special "tooth" that young reptiles use to tear open their eggs from the inside. It usually falls out after the animal's first molt.

EMBRYO
A young animal in the very early stages of development before it is ready to hatch or to be born.

EVOLUTION
Gradual changes in living things that build up over many generations, changing the way they look and the way they live. In reptiles, evolution has produced a huge range of different animals, although some are now extinct.

EXTINCTION
The permanent dying-out of a species of living thing.

FANGS
In snakes, specialized teeth that inject venom. Most fangs are fixed in place, but some fold away when not in use.

FERTILIZATION
The moment when a male and female cell join to produce a new living thing. In reptiles, fertilization occurs before the female lays her eggs or gives birth.

FOSSIL
The remains of something that was once alive, buried and preserved in rock. Fossils provide evidence for reptiles that existed in the past, such as dinosaurs.

HABITAT
The surroundings that an animal normally lives in and that provide it with everything it needs to survive.

HEAT-SENSITIVE PITS
Special pits near some snakes' jaws that detect heat coming from warm-blooded prey.

HERPETOLOGIST
Scientists who specialize in herpetology, which is the study of reptiles and amphibians.

ICHTHYOSAURS
Extinct marine reptiles with streamlined bodies, four flippers, and a fishlike tail.

INCUBATION
The period when a young animal develops inside an egg. Most reptile eggs are kept warm by their surroundings, while a few are warmed by the mother.

Fossil skull of *Cynognathus*

INFRARED
A type of radiation that is invisible to the human eye. Infrared radiation is heat.

JACOBSON'S ORGAN
A special organ located in the roof of the mouth of reptiles and other animals with backbones. Most snakes flick their tongues in and out, using the Jacobson's organ to "taste" scent particles.

KERATIN
A tough substance that gives reptile scales their strength. Keratin is also found in mammals' hooves and hair.

LEAF LITTER
A layer of dead leaves on the ground, often full of small animals. It is an important habitat for some lizards and snakes.

LIGAMENT
A band of tough, fibrous tissue that holds bones together at joints. Snake jaws have unusually elastic ligaments, which lets them stretch wide when swallowing prey.

LIVING FOSSIL
A species that has changed very little over millions of years. Tuatara are examples of living fossils.

MELANOPHORES
Special cells in a reptile's skin that contain pigments, or chemical colors. By moving the pigments, the cells can change the skin's color and patterning.

MOLTING
Shedding the outer skin layer. Most reptiles molt throughout their lives.

MONITOR LIZARDS
A family of lizards that includes the world's largest species, the Komodo dragon. All have heavy bodies; large claws; and long, forked tongues.

NOCTURNAL
Active after dark. Tropical reptiles are often nocturnal, because nights are warm enough for them to stay active.

PALEONTOLOGIST
A person who studies or is an expert in fossil animals and plants.

PARASITE
An animal that lives on or inside another and gets its food from it.

PARTHENOGENESIS
Producing young without mating.

PLASTRON
The lower part of a chelonian's shell. Unlike the upper part (carapace), the plastron is usually flat; it may be hinged so that the animal can seal its head inside.

PLESIOSAURS
Extinct marine reptiles with flipper-shaped limbs and, often, a long neck.

Pterosaur

Wing membrane made of skin

PREDATOR
An animal that hunts others to eat. Most reptiles are predators, feeding on a range of animals. Some kinds—particularly snakes—specialize in eating other reptiles.

PREHENSILE
Able to curl around and grip. Tree snakes and chameleons have prehensile tails.

PREY
Any animal that is food for a predator.

PTEROSAURS
Extinct flying reptiles with long wings.

RECTILINEAR MOTION
A way of moving—used by some snakes—with the body kept in a straight line. Snakes use groups of belly scales as anchors while others lift off the ground.

SCALES
The hard plates covering a reptile's body, made of keratin and joined by bands of flexible skin.

SCUTE
A scale that is reinforced by bone, such as on the bodies of crocodiles.

SYMBIOTIC RELATIONSHIP
A relationship or interaction between two different organisms coexisting in the same environment or habitat.

TERRITORY
The area claimed by an animal (usually the male) to feed and breed in.

ULTRASOUND
Sounds that are too high-pitched for human ears to hear.

VENOM
Toxins produced by snakes and other animals, used in self-defense or for killing prey. Snake venom usually includes a range of substances, such as neurotoxins that attack nerves and anticoagulants that produce internal bleeding.

Vertebrae

VERTEBRA (plural: VERTEBRAE)
The individual bones that make up the backbone, or spine.

VERTEBRATE
Any animal that has a backbone. Vertebrates include fish, amphibians, reptiles, birds, and mammals.

VESTIGIAL LIMB
A leg that has evolved into a very small size and no longer works for moving.

VIVIPAROUS
Giving birth to live young.

WARM-BLOODED
An animal that uses energy from food to keep its body warm. Unlike reptiles, they stay warm all the time.

WEBBED FEET
Feet with toes that are joined together by skin flaps, often found in water-dwelling reptiles.

YOLK
A store of food inside an egg, which lets a young animal develop.

Monitor lizard

Forked tongue

SIDEWINDING
A way of moving used by snakes crossing open sand; the snake repeatedly throws its body diagonally through the air, leaving a series of J-shaped tracks.

SPECIES
The most important level in the classification of living things. Members of a species look like each other and can mate with each other.

Index

AB

adders 22, 53, 69
alligator snapping turtles 32-33, 68
alligators 11, 35
 eggs and offspring 21, 22
 senses 16, 56
amnion 20, 21
amphibians 7, 8, 11, 27, 59
amphisbaenians 65
anapsids 66
Anning, Mary 9
aquatic reptiles 56-57
arboreal reptiles 54-5
babies 20-21, 22-23
Barragán-Paladines, María Elena 27
bipedal movement 52
birds 18, 37, 59, 61, 67
boas 24, 54, 55, 63, 64
 constrictors 40-41
body temperature 14-15, 36
burrowing reptiles 16, 20, 26, 36-37, 51, 60

C

caimans 11, 35, 58
 body structure 12, 24, 50
 eggs and offspring 21, 22
 habitats 49, 56-57
camouflage 30, 33, 48-49, 54
Carboniferous Period 8, 66-67
Carpenter, Charles 18
Cenozoic Era 8, 66-67
chameleons 10, 11, 28-29, 39, 48
 body structure 12, 16, 24
 classification 10, 64
 eggs 20

chelonians 30, 66
 see also tortoises; turtles
classification 10, 64-65
cloacas 13, 37
cobras 10, 24, 58, 63, 65, 69
cold-blooded bodies 6, 14-15
conservation 27, 28, 34, 37, 62-63
constriction 40-41
copperheads 27
corn snakes 26
Cretaceous Period 8, 66-67
crocodiles 10, 14, 21, 35
 diet 22, 38
 eggs 21
 habitats 56, 57, 61, 68-69
crocodilians 10-11, 21, 34, 65
 body structure 12, 37, 50
 habitats 55, 56
 prehistoric 8, 67
 see also alligators; caimans; crocodiles
crocodylomorphs 8
Cynognathus 9

D E F

defenses 46-47, 48-49
dewlaps 18
diet 38-39, 44-45
displays 18-19
ears 17
Edmontosaurus 66
egg-eating reptiles 38, 44-45
egg tooth 23
eggs 6, 20-21, 22-23
evolution 66-67
extinction 68
 conservation 62-63
 prehistoric reptiles 8-9, 66-67
eyes 16, 25, 27, 56

families (classification) 10, 64-65
fangs 26, 41, 42, 49
feet 50-51, 52-53
fish 61
flying reptiles 54, 55, 67
forked tongues 7, 17
fossils 8-9, 66-67
frills 18, 46-47
Fulgione, Domenico 48

G H

Galápagos Islands 21, 30, 31
geckos 11, 16, 29, 48, 50-51, 54, 55
 eggs and offspring 20, 23
gharials 11, 21, 34, 63
Giri, Varad 11
groups (classification) 10, 64-65
habitats 60-61, 62-63, 68-69
 aquatic 56-57
 arboreal (tree-dwellers) 54-55
 burrows 16, 36-37, 60
hippopotamuses 60
Homoeosaurus 36

I J K

ichthyosaurs 67
iguanas 11, 17, 28, 61
 feeding 38, 56
 habitats 68, 69
Irwin, Steve 34
Jacobson's organ 16, 17
jaguars 58
jaws 9, 12, 32-33, 35, 39, 40, 41, 42, 43, 67
Jurassic Period 8, 66-67
keratin 24, 25
kingsnake 18, 26, 41
Komodo dragons 28

L

leatherback turtles 31, 68
legs 50-51, 52-53
ligaments 40
live births 6, 20, 22, 28, 66, 67

lizards 6, 10-11, 28-29, 64-65
 body structure 12, 24, 25, 50, 51
 body temperature 14, 15
 defenses 43, 46, 47
 diet 38, 39, 45, 61
 eggs 21
 habitats 54-55, 57, 69
 movement 52-53
 prehistoric 8, 66
 reproduction 18, 19, 20, 23, 44
 senses 16, 17
 see also geckos; iguanas; skinks
Loch Ness Monster 57
Lonesome George 31

M

mammals 9, 58
matamata turtles 21, 33
mating 18-19, 37
milk snakes 27
molochs 28
mongooses 58, 59
monitor lizards 11, 19, 28
 diet 45, 58
 eggs 20
 legs and feet 50
mosasaurs 66
movement 52-53
mythology 7, 30, 34, 57, 59

O P

ocean habitats 68
offspring 20-21, 22-23
ornithischians 67
Oukkache, Naoual 43
parasites 60, 61
Permian Period 8, 66-67
plesiosaurs 67
predators 58-59
prehistoric reptiles 8-9, 66-67
prey 16, 17, 29, 32, 33, 39, 40, 41, 58-59
pterosaurs 8, 67
pythons 8, 10, 40, 41
 body structure 12-13, 17, 24
 eggs 21

R S

rattlesnakes 25, 41, 42-43
rhinoceroses 60
salamanders 7
sauropods 67
scales 24-25, 46, 50, 54
scutes 24, 57
sea snakes 8, 10, 38, 43, 56
senses 16-17
shells 30-31, 57, 62
sidewinding 15, 53
skeletons 12-13
skin 24-25, 62
skinks 20, 28, 29, 63
 body structure 24, 47, 50
 defenses 47, 49, 60
 diet 38
sloughing 25
slow worms 24-25
snake charmers 17
snake stones 42
snakes 26-27, 63
 body structure 12-13, 15, 24-25, 51
 classification 10, 64, 65
 eggs 20, 22-23
 defenses 46, 49, 58, 59
 diet 38, 40-41, 44-45
 habitats 54-55, 56, 60, 69
 mating 18-19
 movement 53
 prehistoric 8, 66
 senses 16, 17
 venom 42-43
stomachs 13, 38, 44
survival methods 46-47, 48-49
symbiotic relationships 60-61

T

tails 25, 29, 47, 56
teeth 8, 23, 38, 44
 fangs 41, 42
terrapins 30, 31, 57
theropods 67

throat sacs 18
Titanoboa 40
tongues 17, 29, 32, 39
tortoises 30-31, 38, 66
 body structure 13, 50
 eggs 21
 classification 11, 65
 habitats 60, 68, 69
 reproduction 18
tree-dwellers 54-55
Triassic Period 8, 66-67
tuataras 10, 36-37, 65, 67
turtles 13, 30-31, 32-33, 38
 classification 10, 11, 65
 defenses 46, 48
 eggs 21, 23
 habitats 57, 62, 68, 69
 prehistoric 9, 66
 symbiotic relationships 60, 61
Tweats, Harvey 59

V W Y

venomous reptiles 42-43
 snakes 22, 26-27, 40, 42, 43, 49, 58, 65, 69
vertebrae 8, 12-13, 47
vine snakes 27
vipers 10, 15, 42, 49
water-dwellers 56-57
webbed feet 50, 54, 57
Whitaker, Romulus 63
Whitehurst, Tom 59
Wikramanayake, Shanelle 28
yolk 21, 23
young 20-21, 22-23

Acknowledgments

The publisher would like to thank the following people for their help with making the book:
Trevor Smith and all the staff at Trevor Smith's Animal World for their help and enthusiasm; Cyril Walker at the Natural History Museum for pages 8 and 9; Keith Brown, Isolde McGeorge, and Chester Zoo for their kind permission to photograph tuatara; Saloni Singh for the jacket; Hazel Beynon for proofreading; and Elizabeth Wise for the index.

The publisher would like to thank the following for their kind permission to reproduce their images:
(a=above; b=below/bottom; c=center; f=far; l=left; r=right; t=top)

123RF.com: Andrey Gudkov 28cl; **Alamy Stock Photo:** AP Photo / Frank Glaw 10bl, 64crb, blickwinkel / F. Teigler 16clb, blickwinkel / Layer 32bc, Bsip Sa / Jacopin 40clb, Michele Burgess 41crb, Sunny Celeste 49bl, Charles Walker Collection 45br, Chronicle 57tc, James Cresswell 40tr (background), Dorling Kindersley ltd 32-33c, Fotofritz 10br, Vlad Ghiea 22tr, GRANGER— Historical Picture Archive 59crb, The National Trust Photolibrary / John Hammond 34cr, IanDagnall Computing 9bc, Juniors Bildarchiv GmbH / Giel, O. / juniors@wildlife 38tl, Juniors Bildarchiv GmbH / R304 61crb, Ivan Kuzmin 30cb, Michael Mantke 60cl, Jonathan Mbu (Pura Vida Exotics) 48-49c, Minden Pictures / Jeff Foott 58tr, Minden Pictures / Stephen Dalton 57tr, Nature Picture Library 69crb, Nature Picture Library / Ann & Steve Toon 53cr, Nature Picture Library / Daniel Heuclin 62-63c, Nature Picture Library / Georgette Douwma 61tl, Nature Picture Library / Kim Taylor 54cla, Oliver Lucanus / NiS / Minden Pictures 43cra, Burger / Phanie 19r, Roger Harris / Science Photo Library 8tl, RooM the Agency / shikheigoh 28-29c, Nature Picture Library / Anup Shah 38cl, Sibag 14bl, Stephanie Jackson / Australian wildlife collection 19tl, World History Archive 22bc, Nature Picture Library / Wild Wonders of Europe / Zankl 23tr, Zoonar GmbH / Andrey Armyagov 56-57b, Milan Zygmunt 7cra; **Ancient Art & Achitecture Collection:** 34b; **Bridgeman Images:** © British Library Board. All Rights Reserved 30tl; **British Museum (Natural History):** 9c; **Jane Burton:** 25b; **Corbis:** Martin Harvey 68bc, Gary Meszaros / Visuals Unlimited 68cl, Michael & Patricia Fogden

69fbr; **Depositphotos Inc:** artistrobd 48cla; **Dorling Kindersley:** Colin Keates / Natural History Museum, London 20tc, Karl Shone 36-37c, Jerry Young 18bl, Lars Bergendorf 69tc, Hunterian Museum (University of Glasgow) 67cl, Natural History Museum, London 66cr, 66cb, 67c, 67fcl, 70cr, 71cr; Jerry Young—DK Images 67tl, 69bl; **Dreamstime.com:** Matthijs Kuijpers 33t, Wayan Sumatika 46-47c; **Guardian/ eyevine:** Christopher Thomond 59bc; **Mary Evans Picture Library:** 7tr; 17tl; 27tr; 38cr; 43tl; 50-51; 57tc; 58tl; **Domenico Fulgione:** Domenico Fulgione 48bc; **Sally & Richard Greenhill:** 24cr; **Robert Harding Picture Library:** 16t; 47tl; **Getty Images:** Anthony Wallace / AFP 62tl, Alan Tunnicliffe Photography 10-11tc, James L. Amos 37br, Eva Ozkoidi / EyeEm 56cl, Lucy Clark / EyeEm 56tr, Stephen Frink 43c, Justin Sullivan / Stringer 34bl, Mark Conlin / VW PICS / Universal Images Group 31cr, Rodrigo Buendia / AFP / Stringer 31cla, Universal History Archive / Universal Images Group 34cla, Dea Picture Library / De Agostini Picture Library 69tl, Patricio Robles Gil / age fotostock 69crb; **Getty Images / iStock:** GordonImages 37tr, stevegeer 68clb, SteveMcsweeny 62br; **Varad Giri:**

Vaibhav Naik 11br; **The Hindu Archives:** 63br; **naturepl.com:** Daniel Heuclin 6bl, Klein & Hubert 43tc, Barry Mansell 52bl, Alex Mustard 61cra, Tui De Roy 18tl, 20-21c, 61cl, Roland Seitre 42cl; **Naoual Oukkache:** 43ca; **María Elena Barragán-Paladines:** Niñita Sani Lodge / FHGO Files 27bc; **Oxford Scientific Films:** /S. Osolinski 18cla; /Z. Leszczynski 41mr; **Photoshot:** Bill Love 65br; **Science Photo Library:** Bsip / Jacopin 40cl, Craig K. Lorenz 37tc; **Shutterstock. com:** Ryan M. Bolton 46c, Chantelle Bosch 15br, EcoPrint 14r; **Syndication International:** 6cl; **Caryn C. Vaughn:** 18br; **Shanelle Wikramanayake:** Sanoj Wijayasekara 28bc; **Jerry Young:** 67tl, 69bl; **Illustrations by Andrew Macdonald:** 53.

All other images © Dorling Kindersley